D1164230

Principles in Practice

The Principles in Practice imprint offers teachers concrete illustrations of effective classroom practices based in NCTE research briefs and policy statements. Each book discusses the research on a specific topic, links the research to an NCTE brief or policy statement, and then demonstrates how those principles come alive in practice: by showcasing actual classroom practices that demonstrate the policies in action; by talking about research in practical, teacher-friendly language; and by offering teachers possibilities for rethinking their own practices in light of the ideas presented in the books. Books within the imprint are grouped in strands, each strand focused on a significant topic of interest.

Volumes in the Adolescent Literacy Strand

Adolescent Literacy at Risk? The Impact of Standards (2009) Rebecca Bowers Sipe

Adolescents and Digital Literacies: Learning Alongside Our Students (2010) Sara Kajder

Adolescent Literacy and the Teaching of Reading: Lessons for Teachers of Literature (2010) Deborah Appleman

Volumes in the Writing in Today's Classrooms Strand

Writing in the Dialogical Classroom: Students and Teachers Responding to the Texts of Their Lives (2011) Bob Fecho

Becoming Writers in the Elementary Classroom: Visions and Decisions (2011) Katie Van Sluys

NCTE Editorial Board

Jonathan Bush
Barry Gilmore
Sue Hum
Claude Mark Hurlbert
Franki Sibberson
Mariana Souto-Manning
Melanie Sperling
Diane Waff
Shelbie Witte
Kurt Austin, Chair, ex officio
Kent Williamson, ex officio

Becoming Writers in the Elementary Classroom

Visions and Decisions

Katie Van Sluys
DePaul University

RECEIVED
MAY 16 2012
MINNESOTA STATE UNIVERSITY LIBRARY
MANKATO, MN 56002-8419

NCTE

National Council of Teachers of English
1111 W. Kenyon Road, Urbana, Illinois 61801-1096

Staff Editors: Carol Roehm and Bonny Graham

Imprint Editor: Cathy Fleischer

Interior Design: Victoria Pohlmann

Cover Design: Pat Mayer

Cover and Interior Photos: Lindsey Hatton

NCTE Stock Number: 02770

©2011 by the National Council of Teachers of English.

All rights reserved. No part of this publication may be reproduced or transmitted in any form or by any means, electronic or mechanical, including photocopy, or any information storage and retrieval system, without permission from the copyright holder. Printed in the United States of America.

It is the policy of NCTE in its journals and other publications to provide a forum for the open discussion of ideas concerning the content and the teaching of English and the language arts. Publicity accorded to any particular point of view does not imply endorsement by the Executive Committee, the Board of Directors, or the member-ship at large, except in announcements of policy, where such endorsement is clearly specified.

Every effort has been made to provide current URLs and email addresses, but because of the rapidly changing nature of the Web, some sites and addresses may no longer be accessible.

Library of Congress Cataloging-in-Publication Data

Van Sluys, Katie
   Becoming writers in the elementary classroom : visions and decisions / Katie Van Sluys.
       p. cm.
   Includes biliographical references and index.
   ISBN 978-0-8141-0277-0 ((pbk) : alk. paper)
  1. English language—Composition and exercises—Study and teaching (Elementary) 2. Language arts (Elementary) I. Title.
   LB1576.V334 2011
   372.6'044—dc23
                                                    2011016095

LB
1576
.V334
2011

Contents

Acknowledgments vii

NCTE Beliefs about the Teaching of Writing ix

Chapter 1 . . . . Writers for Today and Tomorrow's World 1

Chapter 2 . . . . Articulating a Vision: What We Know and Where
We Can Go 16

Chapter 3 . . . . Making Decisions: Why We Write, What We Write,
and How We Write 27

Chapter 4 . . . . Becoming Aware: Learning to See and Own
Writing Decisions 65

Chapter 5 . . . . Teaching with Intention: Assessment as a Means
to Understand Experiences and Pursue Next Steps 91

Chapter 6 . . . . Reaching Outward: Thinking Together about Visions
and Decisions 114

Postscript . . . . Becoming a Writer 131

Annotated Bibliography 135

Works Cited 139

Index. 141

Author. 145

Acknowledgments

This book is about the visions we hold for young writers as well as the daily work and thinking involved in learning to write well. It is about the deep thinking and decision making that occur each day as intentional teachers puzzle through the rhetoric of dominant educational discourses and the lives, experiences of, and visions for the young people in their classrooms. It is about the decisions young people make—decisions that teach us about learners' current understandings of language and the roles that writing can play in the world. It is about the ongoing thinking and learning of professional organizations, colleagues, communities, and young writers. All of the visions and decisions featured within the covers of this book could not be shared with readers without the teachers and students who graciously open their classrooms, notebooks, files, thinking, and lives to me, one another, and our profession.

I thank the teachers who made contributions to this project. Their willingness to take risks and try out new ideas and possible responses to new (as well as enduring) challenges has offered more possible paths to take as we work with writers. To honor the work of those teachers, whenever possible I've used their real names when referring to their work. For those whose names may not appear, know that your work is also valued and respected. I am truly grateful for the times I've been welcomed into your classrooms and thinking—your tireless efforts are an inspiration to many.

I thank the children who not only shared their best work but also shared their rough draft thinking as they put their life experiences, reflections, concerns, and needs into print. Each day spent with these young people sent me back into the world with energy, enthusiasm, and confidence for what can be.

I thank educational leaders who support intentional and responsive teaching. Specifically, I must thank two principals who are genuine instructional leaders—Megan Stanton Anderson and Mariel Laureano. These women understand young people, curriculum, learning, and how to support teachers so that work with children is meaningful and lasting. Their visions and daily decisions create spaces that support the contributions and ongoing development of professional educators and young learners alike. Being welcome and present in their schools is an honor.

I thank NCTE for its efforts to support and highlight the smart work of educators. The Principles in Practice imprint in particular offers a means to feature educators' everyday work in ways that demonstrate the behind-the-scenes thinking that informs such practice.

I thank the people integral to the actual coming-together of this book—Cathy Fleischer, Lindsey Hatton, and reviewers. Cathy's just-in-time thoughtful writing conferences offered needed insight and important questions that helped shape this book. Lindsey's organizational and photographic skills captured stunning images of children and teachers at work. And colleagues who reviewed this work with intense care offered just the right feedback needed to move the initial manuscript into the book that follows.

I thank Tim, Nancy, Jerri, and the beagles, who are constantly at my side as I write, as well as other friends and family. They are the ones who support all of my efforts to work with schools, teach, write, create, entertain, volunteer, learn, dream, act, and enjoy as well as shape new possibilities for our world. It is my hope that this book invites readers to explore and enact possibilities that can strengthen writing pedagogy and practice for all.

NCTE Beliefs about the Teaching of Writing

Just as the nature of and expectation for literacy has changed in the past century and a half, so has the nature of writing. Much of that change has been due to technological developments, from pen and paper, to typewriter, to word processor, to networked computer, to design software capable of composing words, images, and sounds. These developments not only expanded the types of texts that writers produce, they also expanded immediate access to a wider variety of readers. With full recognition that writing is an increasingly multifaceted activity, we offer several principles that should guide effective teaching practice.

Everyone has the capacity to write, writing can be taught, and teachers can help students become better writers

Though poets and novelists may enjoy debating whether or not writing can be taught, teachers of writing have more pragmatic aims. Setting aside the question of whether one can learn to be an artistic genius, there is ample empirical evidence that anyone can get better at writing, and that what teachers do makes a difference in how much students are capable of achieving as writers.

Developing writers require support. This support can best come through carefully designed writing instruction oriented toward acquiring new strategies and skills. Certainly, writers can benefit from teachers who simply support and give them time to write. However, instruction matters. Teachers of writing should be well-versed in composition theory and research, and they should know methods for turning that theory into practice. When writing teachers first walk into classrooms, they should already know and practice good composition. However, much as in doctoring, learning to teach well is a lifetime process, and lifetime professional development is the key to successful practice. Students deserve no less.

People learn to write by writing

As is the case with many other things people do, getting better at writing requires doing it—a lot. This means actual writing, not merely listening to lectures about writing, doing grammar drills, or discussing readings. The more people write, the easier it gets and the more they are motivated to do it. Writers who write a lot learn more about the process because they have had more experience inside it. Writers learn from each session with their hands on a keyboard or around a pencil as they draft, rethink, revise, and draft again. Thinking about how to make your writing better is what revision is. In other words, improvement is built into the experience of writing.

What does this mean for teaching?

Writing instruction must include ample in-class and out-of-class opportunities for writing and should include writing for a variety of purposes and audiences.

Writing, though, should not be viewed as an activity that happens only within a classroom's walls. Teachers need to support students in the development of writing lives, habits,

NCTE Beliefs about the Teaching of Writing

and preferences for life outside school. We already know that many students do extensive amounts of self-sponsored writing: emailing, keeping journals or doing creative projects, instant messaging, making Web sites, blogging, and so on. As much as possible, instruction should be geared toward making sense in a life outside of school, so that writing has ample room to grow in individuals' lives. It is useful for teachers to consider what elements of their curriculum they could imagine students self-sponsoring outside of school. Ultimately, those are the activities that will produce more writing.

In order to provide quality opportunities for student writing, teachers must minimally understand:

- How to interpret curriculum documents, including things that can be taught while students are actually writing, rather than one thing at a time to all students at once.
- The elements of "writing lives" as people construct them in the world outside of school.
- Social structures that support independent work.
- How to confer with individual writers.
- How to assess while students are writing.
- How to plan what students need to know in response to ongoing research.
- How to create a sense of personal safety in the classroom, so that students are willing to write freely and at length.
- How to create community while students are writing in the same room together.

Writing is a process

Often, when people think of writing, they think of texts—finished pieces of writing. Understanding what writers do, however, involves thinking not just about what texts look like when they are finished but also about what strategies writers might employ to produce those texts. Knowledge about writing is only complete with understanding the complex of actions in which writers engage as they produce texts. Such understanding has two aspects. First is the development, through extended practice over years, of a repertoire of routines, skills, strategies, and practices for generating, revising, and editing different kinds of texts. Second is the development of reflective abilities and meta-awareness about writing. This procedural understanding helps writers most when they encounter difficulty, or when they are in the middle of creating a piece of writing. How does someone get started? What do they do when they get stuck? How do they plan the overall process, each section of their work, and even the rest of the sentence they are writing right now? Research, theory, and practice over the past 40 years has produced a richer understanding of what writers do—those who are proficient and professional as well as those who struggle.

Two further points are vital. To say that writing is a process is decidedly not to say that it should—or can—be turned into a formulaic set of steps. Experienced writers shift between different operations according to tasks and circumstances. Second, writers do not accumulate process skills and strategies once and for all. They develop and refine writing skills throughout their writing lives.

NCTE Beliefs about the Teaching of Writing

What does this mean for teaching?

Whenever possible, teachers should attend to the process that students might follow to produce texts—and not only specify criteria for evaluating finished products, in form or content. Students should become comfortable with prewriting techniques, multiple strategies for developing and organizing a message, a variety of strategies for revising and editing, and strategies for preparing products for public audiences and for deadlines. In explaining assignments, teachers should provide guidance and options for ways of going about it. Sometimes, evaluating the processes students follow—the decisions they make, the attempts along the way—can be as important as evaluating the final product. At least some of the time, the teacher should guide the students through the process, assisting them as they go. Writing instruction must provide opportunities for students to identify the processes that work best for themselves as they move from one writing situation to another.

Writing instruction must also take into account that a good deal of workplace writing and other writing takes place in collaborative situations. Writers must learn to work effectively with one another.

Teachers need to understand at least the following in order to be excellent at teaching writing as a process:

- The relationship between features of finished writing and the actions writers perform.
- What writers of different genres say about their craft.
- The process of writing from the inside, that is, what they themselves as writers experience in a host of different writing situations.
- Multiple strategies for approaching a wide range of typical problems writers face during composing, including strategies for audience and task analysis, invention, revision, and editing.
- Multiple models of the writing process, the varied ways individuals approach similar tasks, and the ways that writing situations and genres inform processes.
- Published texts, immediately available, that demonstrate a wide range of writing strategies and elements of craft.
- The relationships among the writing process, curriculum, learning, and pedagogy.
- How to design time for students to do their best work on an assignment.
- How writers use tools, including word-processing and design software and computer-based resources.

Writing is a tool for thinking

When writers actually write, they think of things that they did not have in mind before they began writing. The act of writing generates ideas. This is different from the way we often think of writers—as getting ideas fixed in their heads before they write them down. The notion that writing is a medium for thought is important in several ways. It suggests a number of important uses for writing: to solve problems, to identify issues, to construct questions, to reconsider something one had already figured out, to try out a half-baked idea. This insight that writing is a tool for thinking helps us to understand the process of drafting and revision as one of exploration and discovery, and is nothing like transcribing from prerecorded tape. The writing process is not one of simply fixing up the mistakes in an early draft, but of finding more and more wrinkles and implications in what one is talking about.

What does this mean for teaching?

In any writing classroom, some of the writing is for others and some of the writing is for the writer. Regardless of the age, ability, or experience of the writer, the use of writing to generate thought is still valuable; therefore, forms of writing such as personal narrative, journals, written reflections, observations, and writing-to-learn strategies are important.

In any writing assignment, it must be assumed that part of the work of writers will involve generating and regenerating ideas prior to writing them.

Excellence in teaching writing as thinking requires that the teacher understand:

- Varied tools for thinking through writing, such as journals, writers' notebooks, blogs, sketchbooks, digital portfolios, listservs or online discussion groups, dialogue journals, double-entry or dialectical journals, and others.
- The kinds of new thinking that occur when writers revise.
- The variety of types of thinking people do when they compose, and what those types of thinking look like when they appear in writing.
- Strategies for getting started with an idea, or finding an idea when one does not occur immediately.

Writing grows out of many different purposes

Purposes for writing include developing social networks; engaging in civic discourse; supporting personal and spiritual growth; reflecting on experience; communicating professionally and academically; building relationships with others, including friends, family, and like-minded individuals; and engaging in aesthetic experiences.

Writing is not just one thing. It varies in form, structure, and production process according to its audience and purpose. A note to a cousin is not like a business report, which is different again from a poem. The processes and ways of thinking that lead up to these varied kinds of texts can also vary widely, from the quick single-draft email to a friend to the careful drafting and redrafting of a legal contract. The different purposes and forms both grow out of and create various relationships between the writer and the potential reader, and relationships reflected in degrees of formality in language, as well as assumptions about what knowledge and experience is already shared, and what needs to be explained. Writing with certain purposes in mind, the writer focuses her attention on what the audience is thinking or believing; other times, the writer focuses more on the information she is organizing, or on her own thoughts and feelings. Therefore, the thinking, the procedures, and the physical format in writing all differ when writers' purposes vary.

NCTE Beliefs about the Teaching of Writing

What does this mean for teaching?

Often, in school, students write only to prove that they did something they were asked to do, in order to get credit for it. Or, students are taught a single type of writing and are led to believe this type will suffice in all situations. Writers outside of school have many different purposes beyond demonstrating accountability, and they practice myriad types and genres. In order to make sure students are learning how writing differs when the purpose and the audience differ, it is important that teachers create opportunities for students to be in different kinds of writing situations, where the relationships and agendas are varied. Even within academic settings, the characteristics of good writing vary among disciplines; what counts as a successful lab report, for example, differs from a successful history paper, essay exam, or literary interpretation.

In order to teach for excellence about purposes in writing, teachers need to understand:

- The wide range of purposes for which people write, and the forms of writing that arise from those purposes.
- Strategies and forms for writing for public participation in a democratic society.
- Ways people use writing for personal growth, expression, and reflection, and how to encourage and develop this kind of writing.
- Aesthetic or artistic forms of writing and how they are made. That is, the production of creative and literary texts, for the purposes of entertainment, pleasure, or exploration.
- Appropriate forms for varied academic disciplines and the purposes and relationships that create those forms.
- Ways of organizing and transforming school curricula in order to provide students with adequate education in varied purposes for writing.
- How to set up a course to write for varied purposes and audiences.

Conventions of finished and edited texts are important to readers and therefore to writers

Readers expect writing to conform to their expectations, to match the conventions generally established for public texts. Contemporary readers expect words to be spelled in a standardized way, for punctuation to be used in predictable ways, for usage and syntax to match that used in texts they already acknowledge as successful. They expect the style in a piece of writing to be appropriate to its genre and social situation. In other words, it is important that writing that goes public be "correct."

What does this mean for teaching?

Every teacher has to resolve a tension between writing as generating and shaping ideas and writing as demonstrating expected surface conventions. On the one hand, it is important for writing to be as correct as possible and for students to be able to produce correct texts. On the other hand, achieving correctness is only one set of things writers must be able to do; a correct text empty of ideas or unsuited to its audience or purpose is not a good piece

NCTE Beliefs about the Teaching of Writing

of writing. There is no formula for resolving this tension. Writing is both/and: both fluency and fitting conventions. Research shows that facility in these two operations often develops unevenly. For example, as students learn increasingly sophisticated ways of thinking (for example, conditional or subordinate reasoning) or dealing with unfamiliar content, they may produce more surface errors, or perhaps even seem to regress. This is because their mental energies are focused on the new intellectual challenges. Such uneven development is to be tolerated, in fact, encouraged. It is rather like strength gains from lifting weight, which actually tears down muscle fibers only to stimulate them to grow back stronger. Too much emphasis on correctness can actually inhibit development. By the same token, without mastering conventions for written discourse, writers' efforts may come to naught. Drawing readers' attention to the gap between the text at hand and the qualities of texts they expect causes readers to not attend to the content. Each teacher must be knowledgeable enough about the entire landscape of writing instruction to guide particular students toward a goal, developing both increasing fluency in new contexts and mastery of conventions. NCTE's stated policy over many years has been that conventions of writing are best taught in the context of writing. Simply completing workbook or online exercises is inadequate if students are not regularly producing meaningful texts themselves.

Most writing teachers teach students how to edit their writing that will go out to audiences. This is often considered a late stage in the process of composing, because editing is only essential for the words that are left after all the cutting, replacing, rewriting, and adding that go on during revision. Writers need an image in their minds of conventional grammar, spelling, and punctuation in order to compare what is already on the page to an ideal of correctness. They also need to be aware of stylistic options that will produce the most desirable impression on their readers. All of the dimensions of editing are motivated by a concern for an audience.

Teachers should be familiar with techniques for teaching editing and encouraging reflective knowledge about editing conventions. For example, some find it useful to have students review a collection of their writing over time—a journal, notebook, folder, or portfolio—to study empirically the way their writing has changed or needs to change, with respect to conventions. A teacher might say, "Let's look at all the times you used commas," or "Investigate the ways you might have combined sentences." Such reflective appointments permit students to set goals for their own improvement.

Teachers need to understand at least the following in order to be excellent at teaching conventions to writers:

- Research on developmental factors in writing ability, including the tension between fluency with new operations or contents and the practice of accepted spelling, punctuation, syntactic, and usage conventions.
- The diverse influences and constraints on writers' decision making as they determine the kinds of conventions that apply to this situation and this piece of writing.
- A variety of applications and options for most conventions.
- The appropriate conventions for academic classroom English.
- How to teach usage without excessive linguistic terminology.

NCTE Beliefs about the Teaching of Writing

- The linguistic terminology that is necessary for teaching particular kinds of usage.
- The linguistic terminology necessary for communicating professionally with other educators.
- The relationship among rhetorical considerations and decisions about conventions, for example, the conditions under which a dash, a comma, a semicolon, or a full stop might be more effective.
- Conventions beyond the sentence, such as effective uses of bulleted lists, mixed genres and voices, diagrams and charts, design of pages, and composition of video shots.
- An understanding of the relationship among conventions in primary and secondary discourses.
- The conditions under which people learn to do new things with language.
- The relationship between fluency, clarity, and correctness in writing development and the ability to assess which is the leading edge of the student's learning now.

Writing and reading are related

Writing and reading are related. People who read a lot have a much easier time getting better at writing. In order to write a particular kind of text, it helps if the writer has read that kind of text. In order to take on a particular style of language, the writer needs to have read that language, to have heard it in her mind, so that she can hear it again in order to compose it.

Writing can also help people become better readers. In their earliest writing experiences, children listen for the relationships of sounds to letters, which contributes greatly to their phonemic awareness and phonics knowledge. Writers also must learn how texts are structured, because they have to create them. The experience of plotting a short story, organizing a research report, or making line breaks in a poem permits the writer, as a reader, to approach new reading experiences with more informed eyes.

Additionally, reading is a vital source of information and ideas. For writers fully to contribute to a given topic or to be effective in a given situation, they must be familiar with what previous writers have said. Reading also creates a sense of what one's audience knows or expects on a topic.

What does this mean for teaching?

One way to help students become better writers is to make sure they have lots of extended time to read, in school and out. Most research indicates that the easiest way to tap motivation to read is to teach students to choose books and other texts they understand and enjoy, and then to give them time in school to read them. In addition to making students stronger readers, this practice makes them stronger writers.

Students should also have access to and experience in reading material that presents both published and student writing in various genres. Through immersion in a genre, students develop an internalized sense of why an author would select a particular genre for a particular purpose, the power of a particular genre to convey a message, and the rhetorical

NCTE Beliefs about the Teaching of Writing

constraints and possibilities inherent in a genre. Students should be taught the features of different genres, experientially not only explicitly, so that they develop facilities in producing them and become familiar with variant features. If one is going to write in a genre, it is very helpful to have read in that genre first.

Overall, frequent conversations about the connections between what we read and what we write are helpful. These connections will sometimes be about the structure and craft of the writing itself, and sometimes about thematic and content connections.

In order to do an excellent job of teaching into the connections of writing and reading, teachers need to understand at least these things:

- How writers read in a special way, with an eye toward not just what the text says but how it is put together.
- The psychological and social processes reading and writing have in common.
- The ways writers form and use constructs of their intended readers, anticipating their responses and needs.
- An understanding of text structure that is fluid enough to accommodate frequent disruptions.

Writing has a complex relationship to talk

From its beginnings in early childhood through the most complex setting imaginable, writing exists in a nest of talk. Conversely, speakers usually write notes and, regularly, scripts, and they often prepare visual materials that include texts and images. Writers often talk in order to rehearse the language and content that will go into what they write, and conversation often provides an impetus or occasion for writing. They sometimes confer with teachers and other writers about what to do next, how to improve their drafts, or in order to clarify their ideas and purposes. Their usual ways of speaking sometimes do and sometimes do not feed into the sentences they write, depending on an intricate set of decisions writers make continually. One of the features of writing that is most evident and yet most difficult to discuss is the degree to which it has "voice." The fact that we use this term, even in the absence of actual sound waves, reveals some of the special relationship between speech and writing.

What does this mean for teaching?

In early writing, we can expect lots of talk to surround writing, since what children are doing is figuring out how to get speech onto paper. Early teaching in composition should also attend to helping children get used to producing language orally, through telling stories, explaining how things work, predicting what will happen, and guessing about why things and people are the way they are. Early writing experiences will include students explaining orally what is in a text, whether it is printed or drawn.

As they grow, writers still need opportunities to talk about what they are writing about, to rehearse the language of their upcoming texts, and to run ideas by trusted colleagues before taking the risk of committing words to paper. After making a draft, it is often helpful for writers to discuss with peers what they have done, partly in order to get ideas from

NCTE Beliefs about the Teaching of Writing

their peers, partly to see what they, the writers, say when they try to explain their thinking. Writing conferences, wherein student writers talk about their work with a teacher, who can make suggestions or re-orient what the writer is doing, are also very helpful uses of talk in the writing process.

To take advantage of the strong relationships between talk and writing, teachers must minimally understand:

- Ways of setting up and managing student talk in partnerships and groups.
- Ways of establishing a balance between talk and writing in classroom management.
- Ways of organizing the classroom and/or schedule to permit individual teacher-student conferences.
- Strategies for deliberate insertions of opportunities for talk into the writing process: knowing when and how students should talk about their writing.
- Ways of anticipating and solving interpersonal conflicts that arise when students discuss writing.
- Group dynamics in classrooms.
- Relationships—both similarities and differences—between oral and literate language.
- The uses of writing in public presentations and the values of students making oral presentations that grow out of and use their writing.

Literate practices are embedded in complicated social relationships

Writing happens in the midst of a web of relationships. There is, most obviously, the relationship between the writer and the reader. That relationship is often very specific: writers have a definite idea of who will read their words, not just a generalized notion that their text will be available to the world. Furthermore, particular people surround the writer—other writers, partners in purposes, friends, members of a given community—during the process of composing. They may know what the writer is doing and be indirectly involved in it, though they are not the audience for the work. In workplace and academic settings, writers write because someone in authority tells them to. Therefore, power relationships are built into the writing situation. In every writing situation, the writer, the reader, and all relevant others live in a structured social order, where some people's words count more than others, where being heard is more difficult for some people than others, where some people's words come true and others' do not.

Writers start in different places. It makes a difference what kind of language a writer spoke while growing up, and what kinds of language they are being asked to take on later in their experience. It makes a difference, too, the culture a writer comes from, the ways people use language in that culture, and the degree to which that culture is privileged in the larger society. Important cultural differences are not only ethnic but also racial, economic, geographical, and ideological. For example, rural students from small communities will have different language experiences than suburban students from comprehensive high schools, and students who come from very conservative backgrounds in which certain texts

NCTE Beliefs about the Teaching of Writing

are privileged or excluded will have different language experiences than those from progressive backgrounds in which the same is true. How much a writer has access to wide, diverse experiences and means of communication creates predispositions and skill for composing for an audience.

What does this mean for teaching?

The teaching of writing should assume students will begin with the sort of language with which they are most at home and most fluent in their speech. That language may be a dialect of English, or even a different language altogether. The goal is not to leave students where they are, however, but to move them toward greater flexibility, so that they can write not just for their own intimates but for wider audiences. Even as they move toward more widely used English, it is not necessary or desirable to wipe out the ways their family and neighborhood of origin use words. The teaching of excellence in writing means adding language to what already exists, not subtracting. The goal is to make more relationships available, not fewer.

In order to teach for excellence, a writing teacher needs understandings like these about contexts of language:

- How to find out about students' language use in the home and neighborhoods, the changes in language context they may have encountered in their lives, and the kinds of language they most value.
- That wider social situations in which students write, speak, read, and relate to other people affect what seems "natural" or "easy" to them—or not. How to discuss with students the need for flexibility in the employment of different kinds of language for different social contexts.
- How to help students negotiate maintenance of their most familiar language while mastering academic classroom English and the varieties of English used globally.
- Control and awareness of their own varied languages and linguistic contexts.
- An understanding of the relationships among group affiliation, identity, and language.
- Knowledge of the usual patterns of common dialects in English, such as African American English, Spanish and varieties of English related to Spanish, common patterns in American rural and urban populations, predictable patterns in the English varieties of groups common in their teaching contexts.
- How and why to study a community's ways of using language.

Composing occurs in different modalities and technologies

Increasingly rapid changes in technologies mean that composing is involving a combination of modalities, such as print, still images, video, and sound. Computers make it possible for these modalities to combine in the same work environment. Connections to the Internet not only make a range of materials available to writers, they also collapse distances between writers and readers and between generating words and creating designs. Print always has a visual component, even if it is only the arrangement of text on a page and the type font.

NCTE Beliefs about the Teaching of Writing

Furthermore, throughout history, print has often been partnered with pictures in order to convey more meaning, to add attractiveness, and to appeal to a wider audience. Television, video, and film all involve such combinations, as do websites and presentation software. As basic tools for communicating expand to include modes beyond print alone, "writing" comes to mean more than scratching words with pen and paper. Writers need to be able to think about the physical design of text, about the appropriateness and thematic content of visual images, about the integration of sound with a reading experience, and about the medium that is most appropriate for a particular message, purpose, and audience.

What does this mean for teaching?

Writing instruction must accommodate the explosion in technology from the world around us.

From the use of basic word processing to support drafting, revision, and editing to the use of hypertext and the infusion of visual components in writing, the definition of what writing instruction includes must evolve to embrace new requirements.

Many teachers and students do not, however, have adequate access to computing, recording, and video equipment to take advantage of the most up-to-date technologies. In many cases, teaching about the multimodal nature of writing is best accomplished through varying the forms of writing with more ordinary implements. Writing picture books allows students to think between text and images, considering the ways they work together and distribute the reader's attention. Similar kinds of visual/verbal thinking can be supported through other illustrated text forms, including some kinds of journals/sketchbooks and posters. In addition, writing for performance requires the writer to imagine what the audience will see and hear and thus draws upon multiple modes of thinking, even in the production of a print text. Such uses of technology without the latest equipment reveal the extent to which "new" literacies are rooted also in older ones.

Teachers need to understand at least the following in order to be excellent at teaching composition as involving multiple media:

- A range of new genres that have emerged with the increase in electronic communication. Because these genres are continually evolving, this knowledge must be continually updated.
- Operation of some of the hardware and software their students will use, including resources for solving software and hardware problems.
- Internet resources for remaining up to date on technologies.
- Design principles for webpages.
- Email and chat conventions.
- How to navigate both the World Wide Web and Web-based databases.
- The use of software for making websites, including basic html, such as how to make a link.
- Theory about the relationship between print and other modalities.

NCTE Beliefs about the Teaching of Writing

Assessment of writing involves complex, informed, human judgment

Assessment of writing occurs for different purposes. Sometimes, a teacher assesses in order to decide what the student has achieved and what he or she still needs to learn. Sometimes, an entity beyond the classroom assesses a student's level of achievement in order to say whether they can go on to some new educational level that requires the writer to be able to do certain things. At other times, school authorities require a writing test in order to pressure teachers to teach writing. Still other times, as in a history exam, the assessment of writing itself is not the point, but the quality of the writing is evaluated almost in passing. In any of these assessments of writing, complex judgments are formed. Such judgments should be made by human beings, not machines. Furthermore, they should be made by professionals who are informed about writing, development, and the field of literacy education.

What does this mean for teaching?

Instructors of composition should know about various methods of assessment of student writing. Instructors must recognize the difference between formative and summative evaluation and be prepared to evaluate students' writing from both perspectives. By formative evaluation here, we mean provisional, ongoing, in-process judgments about what students know and what to teach next. By summative evaluation, we mean final judgments about the quality of student work. Teachers of writing must also be able to recognize the developmental aspects of writing ability and devise appropriate lessons for students at all levels of expertise.

Teachers need to understand at least the following in order to be excellent at writing assessment:

- How to find out what student writers can do, informally, on an ongoing basis.
- How to use that assessment in order to decide what and how to teach next.
- How to assess occasionally, less frequently than above, in order to form judgments about the quality of student writing and learning.
- How to assess ability and knowledge across multiple writing engagements.
- What the features of good writing are, appropriate to the context and purposes of the teaching and learning.
- What the elements of a constructive process of writing are, appropriate to the context and purposes of the teaching and learning.

NCTE Beliefs about the Teaching of Writing

- What growth in writing looks like, the developmental aspects of writing ability.
- Ways of assessing student metacognitive process of the reading/writing connection.
- How to recognize in student writing (both in their texts and in their actions) the nascent potential for excellence at the features and processes desired.
- How to deliver useful feedback, appropriate for the writer and the situation.
- How to analyze writing situations for their most essential elements, so that assessment is not of everything about writing all at once, but rather is targeted to objectives.
- How to analyze and interpret both qualitative and quantitative writing assessments.
- How to evaluate electronic texts.
- How to use portfolios to assist writers in their development.
- How self-assessment and reflection contribute to a writer's development and ability to move among genres, media, and rhetorical situations.

A guideline by the Writing Study Group of the NCTE Executive Committee, November 2004

Chapter One

Writers for Today and Tomorrow's World

Recently, when I was working with a group of educators at a new school, a teacher named Andrea reflected in an introductory activity on the daunting task of raising young people in uncertain and constantly changing times. She also reflected on her fairly new role as a parent and noted how grateful she was that her son would have teachers, as well as parents, in his life. Having teachers in his life, she went on to explain, took some of the pressure off her to make sure she attended to everything her son needed for success in today and tomorrow's world. She ended her introductory vignette by stating that she also realized the flip side of this thinking—that she needed to be the teacher in many other children's lives. She needed to "create a community of learners with understanding and appreciation for the experiences kids bring with them [to school]." She needed to be a teacher who worked responsibly with each and every young person she encountered by "highlighting their successes, focusing on progress, encouraging openmindedness and the consideration of other perspectives, and offering opportunities to experience learning in [rich] ways" to foster student engagement with present and future social life. To meet these challenges, she noted that she needed to actively continue in her own growth and development in the company of colleagues and to "make decisions that are best for [her] and [her] kids," with keen attention to surrounding social life, "because the world is always changing."

For me, Andrea's thinking makes visible several key issues. First, teaching and learning are ongoing, humanistic enterprises. They involve minds and identities. They're primarily about having a vision for the kinds of people needed to participate in society and then about making smart decisions regarding how to foster the growth of such people over time, weighing the many options and "right ways" for what and how we teach. Second, she situates teaching and learning as collective challenges that are not easily solved or accomplished by individuals but instead call for creative responses by groups of collaborators, from the young people who make up classroom learning communities to educator colleagues—and perhaps community members, parents, school administrators, legislators, and so on. And in doing so she points toward the intentionality and impact of decisions made within schools

Ways to Read This Book

Before moving deeper into this book, I thought I'd comment on how you might interact with this text. *Whom you're reading it with* and *why you're reading it* will likely shape *how* you go about your reading.

The company you're reading with will likely vary. You may be reading this book on your own; if so, your responses to it will be an interaction between your thinking and the thinking shared in the book. However, you might instead be reading with a teacher in your own school, or a teacher-friend across town, and you plan to converse regularly about your thoughts and reactions. Or you may be reading this book with a study group that meets either face-to-face or online. You might even be reading this book as part of a class. Whatever the context, I urge you to think about the resources and people whom you might turn to and talk with as you work to connect and extend the thinking laid out here.

Your reasons for reading may influence the pace and the way you tackle reading this book. If you're not well versed in the development of process writing, the overview provided in Chapter 2 may be the context you need. If you're concerned with how you invite kids to actively think about their writing work, the cases and examples in Chapters 3 and 4 may be just where you need to focus. If you and your school community are concerned with understanding and practicing genuine assessment, digging deeply into Chapter 5 should prove helpful.

Thinking about your purposes for reading and the company with whom you're reading might inform how you tackle this text. Chapter by chapter? Reading the introductory chapters for context and then slowing down to digest case by case as you watch the writers in your classroom? As the author, I invite you to read in the way that makes the most sense for you and your colleagues.

while extending her gaze beyond classroom and school walls, noting that in three, five, or twenty years from now, she wants her students to be able to take what they've learned about writing in particular to "communicate their thinking clearly by composing cohesive [texts] in many formats that reflect . . . rich vocabulary and language (and life) experiences." Her thinking calls us to consider how surrounding social worlds and social landscapes impact teaching and learning in schools, and how schools impact the development of our society—present and future.

Reflecting on Andrea's vignette, I can't help but wonder what we *really* know about the contexts in which we and our students currently live. What do we know about the communicative and meaning-making practices alive right now in our students' lives, or even in our own? What do we know about possible futures? Furthermore, what do we know about learning? What are the most effective lines of thinking that can inform our actions and interactions with young people, not only today but in the decades to come? And while Andrea's reflection didn't focus solely on writers and writing instruction, her questions can be easily connected to central issues and concerns on the minds of those who work daily with young writers. What are our visions for writers in today's and tomorrow's worlds? How will we continually transform our practices to align with our beliefs? What curricular decisions will we make as a result of our visions? What decisions will our young writers make in pursuit of these visions? In what ways will local, state, and federal policies impact our work? How can we monitor progress and growth and make changes as we move forward? And what kinds of writers (and people) will we construct?

This book aims to illustrate how teachers of elementary-age writers bring their beliefs to life—through the *visions* they hold for writers, writing, and the world, as well as through the *decisions* they make every day in their classrooms. Taking this stance enables us to (re)claim aspects of our professional practice. As teachers, we're faced with contextual challenges (from external pressures for particular sorts of performance, to curriculum that is set by those outside of our classrooms, to changing demographics, to one-size-fits-all programs, etc.)—pressures that sometimes seem to contradict a vision we hold about teaching. And while each of our local challenges is unique in some ways, we

What to Expect as You Read . . .

You might anticipate that in a book about becoming writers you'll be invited to write—and this book does just that. Periodically, chapters offer direct invitations for you to take time to pause, write, and think deeply about your contexts, experiences, and responses to the ideas raised. At various points in the book, I'll explicitly invite you to record your current and evolving thoughts about beliefs and visions that shape your teaching practices. I encourage you to do this whether you're reading for a class, with a group, or on your own. Returning to earlier thinking always surprises me as I reread the books on my shelves, and I imagine that you too will enjoy seeing the shifts and changes in your own thinking over time.

Remember, reading is always interactive, and talking with text transforms reading from an act of consuming information to using and generating knowledge that can move us all forward.

have this in common: the young people who inhabit our classrooms. Every one of our students deserves opportunities to become a competent, constantly growing writer who uses writing to think, communicate, pose, and solve problems, and who learns not only to write well but also to use writing to create the world he or she wants to live in. While others may continue on the fruitless quest to find uniform curricular answers for teaching writing, in this book I call on teachers to draw on and expand their professional knowledge, to articulate their visions, and subsequently to make decisions that meet the needs of real people living and learning in their classrooms—such that young writers not only learn in our company but also learn to use their skills as writers beyond the walls and timelines of school. In my mind, more important than a specific curriculum or a specific strategy is a focus on the vision we hold and the decisions we make as a result of that vision—this is what should drive teacher practice (see Table 1.1).

Beginning with (a) Vision: Writing, Writers, and the World

Beginning to articulate a vision of what it means to be a writer involves first looking closely at writing, writers, and the world to explore and better understand the real work involved in acts of writing. If I were to make a list of the many ways I've used writing in the last week, for example, my list would include responding to an Evite; writing a thank-you note; updating my to-do list; crafting an email message to colleagues; responding to a survey/questionnaire; translating a permission form; narrating life events on a social networking site; sending a text to update our family on travel progress; drafting a syllabus; creating plans for professional development experiences; IMing to solidify social and work-related plans, including communicating electronically with a librarian regarding a resource issue; and revising an annual report through Google Docs with colleagues. If you were to make a list of the many ways you've used writing recently, you are bound to find overlaps with mine as well as unique demands and interests that arise from your life space. Perhaps you

Table 1.1: Visions and Decisions

Visions	Decisions
• Beliefs you hold about writing and writing well • Imagined skills and practices you understand to be necessary for writers to live, think, and act within and beyond their time in schools • Aspirations for who young writers can become as thinkers, communicators, and participants in our changing world	• Choices you make about what, how, and when to teach or study particular skills, pratices, and genres • Choices writers make about reasons to write, what they write, when they write, how they write

too crafted emails, but maybe you also updated a family scrapbook or webpage or wrote a letter to an insurance company, filled out a form or used writing to reflect on a situation, or drafted a memo or class newsletter.

Our lists, regardless of the exact items, demonstrate the diversity in the ways and reasons we use writing as a tool for living in our world today. They illustrate not only what we write and why we write but also with and for whom we write. When I look over my list, I know that the way I approached writing an annual report for a supervisor in a collaborative fashion with Google Docs is quite different from how I composed an entry on a social networking site that would be read by friends and family. The decisions I had to make as a writer in each instance were varied. For example, when writing the annual report, I had to reread writing composed by others and decide how to match voice and register so that the report would read in a cohesive manner. I had to read carefully for content to make sure my contributions added unique and needed information. When writing for the social networking site, I made decisions about what kind of text was required. For instance, text did not stand alone; photos would help tell the story I wanted to convey. Also, intimately familiar with my audience, I knew I could jump right into the heart of the event without a lot of background experiences that my readers would come to the site already knowing.

What about you? Take a moment to fill out this list yourself (see Table 1.2). What have you written in the past week? And what were some of the decisions you had to make as a writer to complete each piece?

Whether you're reading this book on your own or as part of a class or study group, I again encourage you to take the time to write out your thinking. Putting pen to paper or fingers to keys often leads writers to new discoveries and insights—thinking that often doesn't emerge from "just thinking."

Table 1.2: What Have You Written? What Decisions Have You Made?

What did you write this past week?	As a writer, what were some of the decisions you made?
Report on Google Docs	How to frame my contributions in a way so that others would concur with (and keep) my additions
Texting for social plans	When to use abbreviations and condensed spellings based on my knowledge and assumptions about my audience (the friend I was texting with)

Examining these lists and the decisions underlying the writing in each case suggests to me the importance for us as teachers of exploring how changes in our world impact the ways in which teaching and learning unfold in our classrooms. These lists call us to consider the ways in which changing landscapes demand a shift in our visions regarding what writers need today as well as in the future, and they call us to think about how our visions can be translated into practice in ways that ensure we support writers in becoming wise decision makers capable of responding to the writing demands that unfold in their futures. Good writers increasingly are not those who can follow step-by-step instructions about what writing is (if good writers ever were that!); good writers in the twenty-first century are those who know how to make decisions about what to write, when to write, and how to write: for different purposes, for different audiences, in different genres, and with different technologies.

Let me illustrate what I mean: I've been formally teaching and learning with young learners (ranging in age from five to fifteen), their families, and their communities for a little more than fourteen years. I began my formal teaching career working with fourth-grade readers and writers in the mornings and a class of bilingual kindergartners in the afternoon. In the years that followed, I worked as both a multi-age teacher in a public Minnesota school and a resource teacher at a school in Mexico. My professional inquiries then led me to graduate school, where I worked regularly in multilingual classrooms focused on the literate lives of elementary students across the ages. Now, as a Chicago resident and university professor, I am regularly working with educators and young people in city schools. Reflecting on my experiences, I can already see dramatic shifts in the ways in which people (individually and collectively) use words, texts, images, and design to think, communicate, reflect, inquire, negotiate, and take action. When I was teaching in a primary multi-age classroom in the mid-1990s, my students authored books, wrote reflections on math-thinking processes, took notes, and so on. On one occasion, when left with an unanswered question in our study of outer space and our solar system, we wrote a letter to a kids' science magazine seeking expert advice. Within a year, we were fortunate to read a published response to our letter in a subsequent issue. Given a similar situation today, we could have used a number of different strategies to access more immediate (and perhaps multiple) responses to our unanswered question(s). For example, we might have simply Googled our question, posted it on a science blog, or reviewed FAQs on NASA Quest and submitted our question if it was still unanswered after our review of listed questions and responses.

For teachers, this shift implies huge changes in the decisions we make in the classroom. But it also implies huge changes in the decisions *the writers* in our classrooms need to make. They need to be able to figure out how to choose the best venue for acquiring the information they need. They need to know how to be critical information consumers who can sift through various websites and other resources to find the most current and accurate information. They need to know how to succinctly craft a question that meets submission field constraints if their inquiry is not already addressed. And they need to see themselves as potential participants in such dialogues.

Years later, when I was working with fourth graders to create an interactive brain museum as a way of unifying our inquiries and insights from a shared unit of study, some students crafted an interactive game using HyperStudio software, while others used word-processing software to create labels and extended commentary to accompany their exhibits. In this situation, students worked with more than words. They designed multimedia texts and had opportunities to see firsthand how the museum visitors successfully (or unsuccessfully) made sense of their work. And just this past spring, I worked with fourth-grade writers pursuing writing projects aimed at shifting readers' worldviews and actions. One young person wrote an article about a respected athlete and his perseverance through challenges; another wrote on behalf of an organization she's active in and passionate about; one crafted a letter to a large chain restaurant to inquire about their immense portions and the health of patrons; and still another turned a family story of adoption into an invitation for readers to look beyond the neighborhoods in which they live. In this case, young people's agendas, purposes, genres, and audiences were many given their awareness, passions, and concerns regarding their social environment. Classroom practices can provide evidence of the ways in which changes in our social landscape affect the tools, resources, genres, and practices students draw on and engage with in their writing work.

Shifting Visions

At the start of the second decade of the twenty-first century, we might say that the writing is on the wall. Young people will encounter many changes in the months, years, and decades to come. While change has been a constant across our development as people and societies, the rate of change has intensified. We may be able to anticipate some changes and challenges our students will face; however, we cannot accurately map all they will encounter in their life journeys. They will need to draw on known skills, strategies, and habits of mind to engage in new as well as changing situations. This has significant implications for schools' visions and decisions because schools are critical spaces for shaping what students believe writing is, as well as the kinds of skills and practices they have the potential to develop.

Andrea's introductory vignette, the stories drawn from my life and work, and the margin or mental notes you've made about writing in your life do not stand alone. Many in the literacy community have been calling our attention to the changing nature of literacy and literacies. Barton, Hamilton, and Ivanič (1999) and others emphasize the situated nature of literacy practices and how children experience multiple literacies in their everyday, beyond-school lives. Some children come to school well versed in practices associated with running a family business, others with rich histories of oral language use or experiences with computer-connected learning and communication. Kress (1997) writes that while there are some enduring features of modes of thinking, forms of actions, practices, and values, it is increasingly clear that thinking, composing, and representing are changing. For example, the words we write are often accompanied by images. Likewise, where words are positioned, size and selection of font, and so forth play important roles in shaping the meanings constructed by readers. Bomer, Zoch, David, and Ok's (2010) work with fourth-grade writers, for example, illustrates how young people today with only limited access to technological tools compose networks of texts in which linking, multimodal practices, and design are central to constructing and communicating meaning. Furthermore, the tools we use for composing, both technological and social, shape how, with whom, and why we write. Though some claim that new technologies are detrimental to literacy learning, the truth is that young people today are writing far more frequently than those of previous generations. The Stanford Study of Writing (Haven, 2009) not only points to the volume of writing students are engaged with beyond classroom contexts but also notes that the writing young people engage with in today's world almost always has a genuine audience—they have reasons (beyond grades) and eyes (beyond their teachers') for their writing. While right now that writing is all about texting, IMing, blogging, and social networking, we don't know what the future holds. The only guarantee we have is that change is inevitable. To respond intelligently to such changes, we need to have a clear vision of what we're after in our work as teachers. Who do we want the young people in our classrooms to become? What kind of writers do we want to help construct? And how might we meet our goals?

Articulating *Our/a* Vision

Literacy educator Jerry Harste offers, from my perspective, one of the most useful phrases for engaging in continued growth as professional educators and people. He often begins speaking by stating, "What I believe/think right now is . . . " The beauty of this phrase is that it gives us the right to revise our thinking as we continue to learn and grow. In that spirit, I first invite you to stop and think about what you believe right now about writing, writers, and the world (see Invitation 1.1). Then I offer windows into the visions of others—mine and those of other teachers—visions that are, as Harste says, "right now." By doing so, I hope to identify a point of departure for reading the possible decisions, practices, and actions

---

Invitation 1.1: Current Visions for Writing, Writers, and Writing Instruction

Take time to reflect on and record your current vision. *Right now, this is what I believe about writing, writers, and writing instruction:*

---

included in this book and to make connections with possibilities in other (including your) classrooms. When I posed these same questions to elementary faculty with whom I have worked, here is what some of them said:

What I Believe Writing Is

- personal, valuable, and vital (Meg, teacher, grade 1)
- most meaningful for students when they can choose what they write about (Jennifer, bilingual teacher, grade 3)
- an ever-changing and evolving process (Dena, teacher, grade 3)
- creative (Andrea, transitional bilingual teacher, grades 3 and 4)
- part of the human/community experience (Kimberly, media specialist)
- an opportunity to explore who you are and [to] communicate your thinking in unique, creative, informative, and educated ways (Stephanie, bilingual teacher, grade 1)

Who I Believe Writers Are

- people who come in different shapes and sizes hence bringing different backgrounds to the paper (Andrea, bilingual coordinator, preK–8)
- empowered through choice (Linda, teacher, grade 6)
- communicators (Aubrey, teacher, kindergarten)
- something everyone can become (Trish, teacher, grade 1)

What I Believe about Writing Instruction

- It should include practice (Jennifer, bilingual teacher, grade 3)
- Instruction should attend to the reason why we write before teaching the hows (Jay, teacher, grade 4)
- It should include teacher engagement in writing (Dena, teacher, grade 3)
- It should encourage risk taking, invite writers to try new things, and see mistakes as part of learning (Linda and Michael, teachers, grade 6)
- Too often it is systematic and formulaic (Andrea, transitional bilingual teacher, grades 3 and 4)

When I accepted the same invitation, this is what I came up with: For me, writing is a tool for thinking and communicating issues and ideas that matter to us and to the world. Young people in our classrooms need to be flexible, adaptable problem solvers capable of navigating change with confidence and grace. They need to be regular writers, well versed in diverse tools and practices for writing well, and know that they can modify tools and practice as contexts and needs change. They need to have a known relationship with the purpose of and audience for their writing. And they need to be participants in instruction—people who are well aware of the decisions they make and how their decisions impact their growth and development as they use writing to reflect, remember, and act.

My vision isn't something I've developed on my own; rather, it's influenced by the contexts in which I live, think, and work. I'm betting that the same is true for you. Often, surrounding discourses shape what we think about writing, writers, and instruction: for example, standardized testing discourses that prescribe essay structures; teacher training discourses that emphasize teaching narrative, expository, and persuasive writing; or discourses about curriculum as packaged programs or scripts versus curriculum as a course of experiences and a space that includes not just what is to be learned but also conditions and practices that shape how learning transpires and how people develop (Nieto & Bode, 2008). Furthermore, what we read and who we think with also help to shape our visions. For me, the National Council of Teachers of English (NCTE) plays a critical role in my thinking within this book and beyond. Their perspectives regarding what it means to live a literate life in the twenty-first century, as well as what it means to teach writers in contemporary contexts, merit specific attention in order to understand my stance and perhaps to help you articulate your own.

NCTE's Current Vision

NCTE, as a professional organization, pulls together the research of many literacy educators to capture our current best thinking and create policies, definitions, and belief statements aimed at influencing local and national policies, professional development opportunities, and daily classroom practices. From their work with 21st century literacies, to their work with assessment, to their work with writing, NCTE publishes many policy documents that center on putting forth a public vision that reflects the best of what we know about how to teach and learn the English language arts. For many of us, these policies unite what we already know and believe; for others, these policies and positions offer new ways of thinking forged from research and practice in the field. In either case, these resources help provide a starting point from which we can articulate our visions and our beliefs and then work together to make decisions about our practices.

This book builds on a particular document, *NCTE Beliefs about the Teaching of Writing*, a collection of eleven principles aimed at guiding curricular decisions and practices, written by and for teachers. Its genesis and organization emphasize that teaching is anchored first in a vision—who do we want writers to be? What habits of mind or ways of being must writers possess or embody to be successful today and well beyond tomorrow? The document then breaks down NCTE's shared vision into component principles or beliefs. It is from these principles that communities of learners, through regular reflective work, can bring their beliefs to life.

Reading NCTE's Beliefs

Recently, teacher colleagues and I spent time discussing and assessing our current beliefs and practices through a three-step process. As I talked with teachers, I asked that they first describe their current vision for writers, writing, and the world, just as I asked you to do in Invitation 1.1. I then asked that they take time to describe current instructional and learning practices in their classroom. At this time, I invite you to do the same (see Invitation 1.2). After making notes about our current beliefs and practices, teachers and I then embarked on the third step: reading and rereading the *NCTE Beliefs about the Teaching of Writing*, documenting how this set of beliefs connects to our own beliefs and practices. (You might want to do the same, if you haven't already. The full NCTE statement is reprinted in the front of this book, and a short summary can be found inside the back cover.)

We structured our conversation using this three-step process as a means of putting to paper what came immediately to our minds—those reflections and thoughts of the first two steps that, when we looked back at them, did not always fully represent our best thinking about writing and writers because they were too often shaped by immediate contexts or experiences. Therefore, taking time for the third step—reading the NCTE belief statement—helped us step back from the daily demands of our professional roles to really think about what we believe and how our beliefs relate to the ongoing choices we make. As teachers read the belief

Invitation 1.2: Current Writing Practices

Current vision for writing, writers, and the world (see Invitation 1.1)

Right now, this is what I believe about writing, writers, and writing instruction:

Current practices

Right now, this is how I teach writing and writers:
[What does it look like, sound like, feel like when student writers are engaged in work? What kinds of work are writers pursuing? What are teacher responsibilities? What are student responsibilities? What are writers learning? How are they learning it?]

statement, I noticed most heads nodding in agreement. The teachers' marginal notes and side commentary included reflections about how their own practices relate to specific beliefs and/or how their hopes for growing their practice relate to specific points made in the document. For example, when they read, "Writing has a complex relationship to talk," teachers reflected on the need to be better at conferring. "People learn to write by writing" and "Writing is process," followed by a detailed explanation of what that means from an NCTE perspective, pushed readers to reflect on the need to rethink practices in their own classrooms, such as how much time we offer our students for writing and what a process model of writing means in their specific classroom contexts.

Using this document as a catalyst for further discussion (but, more important, using it as a tool to build on teachers' beliefs and practices) led us to dialogue about areas for growth and how to better align classroom practices with beliefs. A few days after initial reads of this document, Dena noted that she, like NCTE, believed that "Writers learn to write by writing," and went on to connect this statement with thinking about life in her classroom. She explained that, in previous years of teaching, writing in her classroom had gone "down the tubes" by about January.

When asked what she meant, she talked about the writers' notebooks on which she based her writing instruction and how students lost interest, energy, and enthusiasm with their notebooks, and how the volume of writing diminished as the year progressed.

While there are many strategies on how to fill notebooks with student words, our conversation turned from a focus on a particular tool to a discussion more grounded in visions, principles, and practice—in other words, *Why notebooks?* Before encouraging Dena to make changes in classroom practice, we realized we needed to be grounded in why we were advocating for a particular tool. What did we think this tool and associated practices could offer writers? How did such practices impact writers' skills and identities? Through dialogue we agreed that writer's notebooks could allow students a space both to develop thinking and to write in volume—hence helping them learn to write by writing. Notebooks could be places that encourage writers to explore issues, ideas, and events on paper. Notebooks could also encourage writers to be flexible, to play with thinking, and to learn to see entries from different perspectives. But this doesn't just happen. It requires supportive contexts and teaching—from adults and peers. Given Dena's newly articulated clarity about her beliefs about writers, she was able to form a goal for her work with writers in the coming year. Specifically, she decided not only that notebooks needed ongoing attention throughout the year, but also that her students needed to be privy to why they were using notebooks and how their engagement with notebooks was something that could help them learn to write better and differently—*if* they wrote regularly and tried new ways of engaging with writing, thinking, and the world. And she began to make plans to pursue this goal in her teaching.

An immersion in *NCTE Beliefs about the Teaching of Writing* and reflection on their professional knowledge helped Dena and the other teachers both articulate their own visions and reconsider some of their teaching practices. I invite you to try this as well by adding on to the chart you've begun to develop and by talking with other teachers or colleagues about what you're noticing (see Invitation 1.3).

The heart of this book is about moving from documents about stated beliefs and/or our own teaching philosophies to well-aligned actions and goals related to potential areas for growth. Decisions do (and should) follow from visions.

Making Decisions: Matching Visions and Actions

Dena's story is not an isolated one. In many interactions with teachers, when I inquire about ideal visions for writers in their care and what they need to bring their visions to life, teachers share responses that range from a need for greater awareness about how writing practices genuinely unfold in real writing lives, to the need

Invitation 1.3: Current Connections

Current vision for writing, writers, and the world (see Invitation 1.2)

Right now, this is what I believe about writing, writers, and writing instruction:

Current practices (see Invitation 1.2)

Right now, this is how I teach writers and writing:
[What does it look like, sound like, feel like when student writers are engaged in work? What kinds of work are writers pursuing? What are teacher responsibilities? What are student responsibilities? What are writers learning? How are they learning it?]

Connections with NCTE's current thinking

Right now, this is how I see the ideas articulated in **NCTE Beliefs about the Teaching of Writing** *connecting to my current vision and practices:*

for support in making decisions that align with beliefs (versus accepting inherited practices that often run counter to teachers' actual visions).

As educators, we first need clarity about what we believe—in other words, we need vision. We need to know what we're working toward so that we monitor our progress en route. We need to articulate our own vision and think about what beliefs help form the basis of that vision—whether it comes from an NCTE document or another source. In the chapters to come, you will be invited to watch how this process has unfolded for a number of teachers as they work to achieve quality writing instruction, taking into account current local and global challenges and changes regarding what it means to become a successful writer. You will be invited to join these teachers who are committed to better living their visions for young writers through everyday decision making. And, after examining examples of classroom practices and the thinking that informs teachers' as well as writers' decisions, you'll be asked to revisit your vision and think about how these experiences influence the current and potential decisions you make regarding young writers' lives.

In the chapters to come, we will dig deeper into our visions by first looking at how historical and current efforts within our profession and beyond inform what we believe is possible when it comes to learning to write well. Chapter 2 provides a brief overview and context with which to better understand where thinking about writing pedagogy has been, how it has changed over time, and how the challenges we face today are intimately tied to particular histories and understandings of writers, writing, and writing instruction. Chapters 3 through 6 are the heart of this book because they feature ideas, experiences, thinking, visions, and decisions made by teachers and young writers alike. These chapters unpack thinking and suggest possibilities for how educators might approach the challenging work of encouraging and supporting young writers.

In Chapter 3, we will look closely at specific classrooms to make visible the range of decisions that teachers and young writers make as they engage in everyday efforts to become strong teachers and writers. Children and teachers featured in Chapter 3 have made a habit of talking about their thinking and work; they are experienced in articulating what they do and why they do it. However, they didn't arrive in their respective schools with explicit understandings of what they do and why. They learned these things. Chapter 4 also uses lively case studies to explore how we can help young people identify the decisions they make and how their decisions affect their growth as writers. The only way we can know how we are growing and developing is through the ability to mark and monitor progress so that teaching and learning experiences provide writers with just the right next step; therefore, Chapter 5 looks specifically at assessment and how we can craft practices to meet teacher and learner needs. And because we don't and can't work in isolation, Chapter 6 explores how we can move beyond our classroom walls to help others come to know and understand why we do what we do and how classroom activities impact people—people who are writers and decision makers, people whose many future decisions will help shape our collective social world.

As the book comes to a close, you'll be invited to revisit your visions, think about what is most pressing in your contexts and lives, and begin to articulate your intentions for shaping writing experiences so that writers write, writers understand the power of writing, and writers use writing well to accomplish the work needed today, as well as to meet the challenges of tomorrow.

Chapter Two

Articulating a Vision: What We Know and Where We Can Go

As I wrote in the last chapter, I believe it is vital for us as teachers to think hard about our vision for our teaching. It's important as well for us to articulate how our classroom practice connects to that vision. And, as we also saw in that chapter, it is important to turn to the work of others like NCTE to see how our vision and practice connect to what thoughtful current research tells us about writing pedagogy. In this chapter, I want to further that line of thinking, suggesting that we also need to understand how our current knowledge grows both from a history of efforts to shape meaningful writing instruction and practice and from a litany of contemporary challenges that impact what we do.

Knowing more about where we, as a community of literacy educators, have traveled can help us better refine our current approaches to teaching and learning. This understanding can help us situate our knowledge in the larger conversations that have been taking place over the last few decades and, by doing so, realize that we are not alone in the challenges we face.

Writing Research and Practice: Where We've Been and What We Know Right Now

When I look back on the history of writing pedagogy—a complex and rich history that covers hundreds of topics and issues—I'm struck by two major developments that have influenced my work as a writing teacher who is most interested in the development of elementary-age writers. The first is one familiar to most teachers, perhaps the most famous of the changes in how writing has been taught: what's commonly known as the process movement. At its simplest, this movement has helped writing instruction move from explorations of product exclusively to a focus on the processes involved during writing.

Of course, we know that even a general acceptance of a process approach to writing doesn't mean the same thing to all educators. For some, a process approach to teaching writing is a naturalistic approach in which writers freely engage in work of their own choosing. In a school context, this is sometimes envisioned as a free-for-all in which kids and teachers are on their own and the nature of student engagement in writing practices leads to growth and new understandings. For others, including many textbook producers, process is translated into a prescriptive, linear formula (of brainstorming, prewriting, drafting, revising, and editing) for producing something—generally a paper or a story (Pritchard & Honeycutt, 2006). Some who align themselves with a process approach to writing believe that for writers, especially struggling writers, to take on more sophisticated behaviors, they require direct strategy instruction (Graham, 2006) and direction on how to engage at various steps in an already articulated process. Still others think of process in relationship to workshops in which lectures are minimal, small-group work is integral to teaching and learning, and engagement in genuine writing and problem-solving practices is necessary (Boscolo, 2008).

The second development that has influenced my work as well as the work of many other teachers is the increased focus on the social and cultural dimensions of language learning and writing practices (Edelsky, 1989; Gee, 1996; Heath, 1983; Kajder, 2010; Weiser, Fehler, & González, 2009). Students learn differently than adults, this research tells us, in part because the contexts, circumstances, and experiences of their lives outside of school necessarily impact their ways of learning in school. Anne Haas Dyson (1993, 1997), for example, has invited educators to closely attend to the social work of composing, looking specifically at how oral and written language practices can, when allowed, draw from an array of resources and make visible different kinds of writers. Students highlighted in her work illustrate what is possible when kids use their own lives and language resources to compose songs, create comics, and craft written innovations that reflect their lives. Furthermore, research demonstrates how what kids can do changes when opportunities to write are connected to topics in which they have much to say and when teaching respects the life and language resources they bring to schools (Anderson, 2008; Laman & Van Sluys, 2008). Working from the premise that literacy, including writing, is always and everywhere social, educators like Lee Heffernan (2004) and Randy Bomer and Katherine Bomer (2001) have shown through their work with young people how writing is more than mere communication; it's a mode of social action. And when classrooms invite, scaffold, and support acts of writing that reflect the genuine social realities and concerns of students, ranging from narratives exploring social inequities (Heffernan & Lewison, 2003) to new possibilities for action (Bomer & Bomer, 2001), we see shifts in how young writers engage with writing and real audiences. And we see as well how they use available tools to communicate their thinking in ways that reach well beyond writing solely for teachers' eyes.

Writing and Instruction in the Classroom

In thinking specifically about how these understandings of the writing process and children's lived experiences prior to and beyond schooling have played out with regard to decisions and practices in elementary schools, I, along with many others, have been influenced by communities of writers and educators such as Ralph Fletcher, Donald Graves, Don Murray, Kathy Short, Jerome Harste, Carolyn Burke, Carole Edelsky, and Danling Fu, to name just a few. These and many other authors have contributed greatly to the history of elementary writing pedagogy. Though their ideas have grown and changed (remember Harste's reminder to note "This is what I think right now"), certain underlying themes have remained constant and thus constitute the best of what we know about how young writers work.

Focusing on Writing, Workshops, and Authoring Cycles

I first met Ralph Fletcher during my early years of teaching as my primary team of teaching colleagues decided to read *What a Writer Needs* (1992) as a study group text. In the opening pages, Fletcher emphasizes that teachers need to know teaching, know students, as well as know something about writing itself. In this book, he draws from his experiences as a writer to focus on the craft of writing. Recognizing that becoming a writer is about more than producing strong leads or clear transitions, Fletcher and others began to look more broadly at writers' processes and to operationalize what a process approach to teaching writing might look like in classrooms. If we trace the thinking of these educators across the last two decades, we can see shifts and developments in how process orientations to writing instruction in elementary classrooms have developed over time. As a teacher, I was drawn to these ideas, and as a result I began attending to writing differently: in essence, I began to read like a writer and to take note of how writers develop a sense of place, how they begin and end stories, how they create characters, how they make arguments, and so on.

Lucy Calkins, an important voice in the development of elementary teachers' understanding of writing pedagogy, continues to press for children's active and consistent engagement with writing, calling them to be authors, to craft and share text, and to "be part of the struggle to put something vital into print" (1986, p. 8). In the second edition of *The Art of Teaching Writing* (1994), she emphasized that to write well, writers should not begin with the struggle of drafting, but rather with an awareness of how they live in the world. She taught us that there are many reasons to write, including to make sense of our lives, and she underscored the need to care about what we're writing. Along with others like Donald Graves (1983, 1994), another important voice in the field, Calkins highlighted the need to let children lead and reminded us that good instruction is aligned with student needs. Together, Graves and Calkins have helped us to see the powerful ways in which young people use writing as a tool to communicate thinking about their worlds—and through their engagement in actual writing, how they grow as writers.

The work of Graves and Calkins not only offered us insight into writers' processes and writers' craft but also introduced structures and practices for teaching. While recognizing the complexities and uncertainties of writing, Calkins (1994) offered simple and predictable structures, noting however that "*[h]ow* we structure the workshop is less important than *that* we structure it" (p. 188). She and others (Anderson, 2000; Atwell, 1987, 1998; Bomer, 1995; Ray & Laminack, 2001) named mini-lessons, time for writing, peer and teacher conferences and response groups, and share sessions and celebrations as important elements of writing workshop practices. Building on foundations laid by Calkins, Graves, Fletcher, and others, Katie Wood Ray and colleagues (Ray & Laminack, 2001; Ray & Cleaveland, 2004; Ray & Glover, 2008) have unpacked the methodologies often used in writing workshops. Ray continues to offer possible ways to bring writing workshops to life in classrooms but notes the possibility of multiple paths to common destinations. Together, this later work invites teachers to craft focused lessons and engage in writer-to-writer conversations, and it invites kids to use their lived experiences as a primary resource when composing.

Around this same time, Harste and Short (1988) invited teachers to think about creating classrooms for authors, and later for authors and inquirers (Short & Harste, 1996). They offered us authoring and inquiry cycles as ways to create curriculum that meets students' needs, reminding us that curriculum is about meaning making that begins with what is known and then builds on current life experiences, seeking new thinking, perspectives, and experiences to shape literacy lessons that move all learners forward. These frameworks, based on what we know about literacy and learning, illustrate recursive processes and intersecting pathways in learning to write, read, think, and inquire. Their work not only emphasized the role of talk and social relationships involved in acts of writing but also provided images of writing interactions in classrooms that are anchored in well-articulated belief systems.

As I look over this body of work, I am struck by the implicit, and at times explicit, connections between the theories, beliefs, and understandings that teachers hold about writing and writers and their practices. Short and Harste (1996), for example, make a clear connection between teachers' experiences in unpacking the thinking behind particular classroom engagements and how such reflections lead to particular actions. For example, one teacher featured in Short and Harste's *Creating Classrooms for Authors and Inquirers* (1996) decided to use science journals in her classroom. When she took the time to examine exactly how students were using the journals, she began to see the greater potential of these texts—as places for much deeper thinking, rather than as mere tools for recording observations. This teacher moved from a focus on a particular classroom strategy or modality for writing to seeing this writing within a larger construct of beliefs about how students learn to become thoughtful people through thoughtful writing practices.

Focusing on Social Dimensions of Language Learning

A second focus of research in elementary writing pedagogy has attended to the writer herself in her contextual fullness. As Ray and Laminack (2001) state, "[t]he products themselves are not nearly as significant as the child standing behind each one" (p. 3). Educators have studied how writers live, compose, and communicate their thinking, learning that differences in home environments, expectations, and experiences greatly affect how students learn to write. One particular emphasis of the past few years has been on the unique needs of writers new to English. Work with English language learners offers counternarratives to the erroneous belief that oral fluency or grammatical knowledge in English must precede expression of ideas and thinking (Fu, 2003, 2009; Franklin, 1989). Rather, to help young writers new to English express and explore complex meanings, these authors suggest strategies such as combining the use of text and image, inviting use of the learner's native language, asking learners to write as a means of helping them read in their new language, and honoring emergent knowledge of English since learners often are thinking more than their expressive English may initially suggest (Edelsky, 1986; Fu, 2003, 2009; Samway, 2006; Van Sluys, 2005).

Lorraine Wilson (2006) furthers this thinking, explaining that school programs and practices "impact who students become and the lives they lead" (p. xiii). She goes on to write that "it's only when we have identified a particular worldview or vision for the world's people that we can set about planning a curriculum that will turn this vision into reality" (p. xiii).

Connecting Visions with Worldviews

Theories, beliefs, and understandings, it's clear, are tied to more than personal perspectives and classroom activity. Worldviews we're familiar with and subscribe to influence what we sponsor as well as what we ignore in our classrooms (Wilson, 2006). For example, when inviting young people to engage in a study of poetry, one teacher's vision might focus on the structure of haiku or sonnets and include asking kids to write poetry following structural requirements. In contrast, another teacher might see poetry study as addressing the potential of poetry to reflect on the world and call for change, and therefore ask students to read and then compose poetry to reflect this way of thinking. These visions emerge not only from the teacher's experiences with poetry but also from the work of poets in the world and the discourses surrounding poetry instruction in which the instructor has been immersed. Here's what I mean: If you have been a regular reader of Naomi Shihab Nye's (2005, 2008, 2010; Nye & Maher, 2005; Nye & Yaccarino, 2000) work, you know the power of short lines and stanzas to capture big ideas in small spaces. If you have worked closely with learners new to English, you know that this genre can invite deep thinking even when English language skills are emergent (Barbieri, 2002; Van Sluys & Reinier, 2006). But if you look to poetry instruction idea books, form tends to trump meaning—suggesting that learning and following the forms of acrostics, haiku, limericks, and the like constitute the study of writing poetry. So when we as teachers construct a vision of what we might do in our classrooms, we're influenced by what we read, what we hear, and what we've experienced. This stance is echoed in Randy and Katherine Bomer's (2001) work with reading and writing for social action in which they address a dominant perspective in elementary writing classrooms that values and welcomes personal story writing centered on birthdays and family celebrations while shutting out opportunities for young writers to engage with injustices within and through writing practices.

What I've summarized here is but a brief glimpse of where we've been and how the work of these educators and many others has taught us that all elementary students can write well given time, genuine opportunities, and support. Young writers, like their more experienced counterparts, have unique processes. Their processes of thinking and composing are not solitary—writers draw on their experiences with others (e.g., family, movie characters, community, classmates), sometimes silently and sometimes through lively conversation or research with distant (but real) others. Work to date has emphasized the centrality of meaningful writing—in which writers write for personal and social purposes, make choices about the ideas they pursue, and decide how best to communicate their thinking through the particular language(s) and other modalities or genres best suited for a given task. We've learned about the connections between reading lives and writing lives, that how we write is often connected to what we read, and that our use of conventions influences how readers of our work consume our thinking and ideas. And we know that following our students' needs closely is intimately tied to effective instruction. If you think back to *NCTE Beliefs about the Teaching of Writing*, you'll hear echoes of this work in NCTE's thinking and perhaps in your own. Knowing where thinking in the field has grown from, as well as where your own thinking grows from, is essential in formulating plans for where you're heading, in terms of both larger goals for writers and writing curriculum as well as daily instructional decisions.

Contemporary Contexts and Challenges: Worldviews, Discourses, and Our Decisions

As I've noted several times already, we do not shape our views of the world alone. Rather, surrounding discourses influence how we come to see the world—and in this case, writing, writers, and writing instruction. Educational policies that include the tracking of yearly progress via test scores; published programs that identify steps in *the* writing process and associated assignments and activities; school policies that state all writing on display must be conventional or in a particular language; schools with widespread commitment to writing workshops; principals who structure schedules with uninterrupted blocks of time for literacy learning; classrooms that post their thinking about school issues with students using their emergent writing skills in English and other languages—all such conditions play a role in how we construct how the world "is" and how we imagine possibilities for the future. And while many of these ways of seeing literacy learning may be familiar, it is highly probable that some discourses and ways of seeing are more dominant than others (see Figure 2.1).

As discourses develop, so too do responses. We might, for example, find ourselves enacting what I call "inherited practices"— doing things we don't necessarily believe in but have been told to do by someone else. Or we may respond to accountability discourses as quests to find *the* answer, perhaps in the form of a program, that will "help all kids learn." While we know that kids and contexts vary, in many places this search for the universal panacea has introduced the notion of writing workshop to more and more classrooms—in some cases by choice and in others by mandate. In places where educators are well versed in process approaches, they

---

Figure 2.1: Constructing *our* vision: What shapes and informs our thinking.

- Understanding policy and belief statements (like the *NCTE Beliefs about the Teaching of Writing*)
- Reading the work of experts in the field
- Studying and learning with a variety of authors, writers, journalists, and bloggers, either face-to-face or virtually
- Reflecting on our own writing practices
- Thinking (and rethinking) about inherited practices
- Considering individual experiences and background
- Recognizing challenges and conditions in local contexts
- Watching our students closely and carefully

---

are often able to create workshops in their classrooms based on a firm understanding of how such a structure will help them create the sorts of writers the world needs. In other contexts, structures and lessons are followed without an informed knowledge base or a vision for where such teaching might lead. And in these cases, writing workshop is less about student writers learning to make decisions as writers and more about students learning to follow a static process. (It needs to be said that this scenario, while less than ideal, has in many cases introduced writing into some classrooms where writing, in the past, may have meant handwriting practice or isolated grammar exercises. In some cases, it has created the space for professional educators to develop their understandings of what it means to become a writer, study what is known about developing writers, and begin to make decisions that can lead to the construction of more reflective, problem-solving writers. But a word of caution is also important: this stance on workshop approaches might also mean that such spaces have been designed as sites of rehearsal for tested genres of writing, taking the decisions out of the hands of students and teachers. So using the term *writing workshop* is not in itself sufficient to guarantee quality interactions or meaningful learning.)

Take a moment to think about what has informed your vision of writers and writing instruction thus far. Building on the invitations offered in Chapter 1, add to the chart you've already begun to develop, specifically asking yourself what has influenced your vision and practice: what books you've read, what practices you've inherited, what you've observed in the students you've taught, and what you've noticed about your own writing (see Invitation 2.1).

Worldviews and larger discourses about what it means to be a writer affect more than just educators. We might be working in communities in which some young people walk into our classroom yearning for new notebooks, or in which students number the lines on their papers and beg the teacher to assign topics and "tell them how far to go" (i.e., how many lines they *have* to write). We might

Invitation 2.1: Current Writing Practices and Connections

Current vision for writing, writers, and the world (Invitation 1.1)

Right now, this is what I believe about writing, writers, and writing instruction:

Current practices (Invitation 1.2)

Right now, this is how I teach writers and writing:
[What does it look like, sound like, feel like when student writers are engaged in work?
What kinds of work are writers pursuing? What are teacher responsibilities? What are
student responsibilities? What are writers learning? How are they learning it?]

Connections with NCTE's current thinking (Invitation 1.3)

Right now, this is how I see the ideas articulated in NCTE Beliefs about the Teaching of Writing *connecting to my current vision and practices:*

Constructing your vision: What shapes and informs your thinking?

***Right now, the most important influences in why I teach writing the way I do
are . . .***
***[Ask yourself about the reading you've done, the inherited practices in your
teaching context, your observations of students, and your own experiences and
practices as a writer.]***

be working in monolingual, bilingual, and/or multilingual contexts in which our students may or may not have had the support they need to develop print-based literacy skills across the language(s) they speak.

Given the diversity of our educational settings, even the best-designed lessons cannot simply be passed on with guaranteed success. As educators, we need to develop well-grounded visions about our world and the writers and people it needs while keeping our eyes and ears wide open to the conversations and thinking that surround us. We need to blend the local, contextual, and situated needs with our visions for the kind of writers and thinkers we want young people to become. We need to see ourselves not merely as implementers, but as people who have the knowledge and experience to design and redesign curriculum (Cazden et al., 1996) through the daily decisions we make. Our students also need visions and opportunities to make decisions so that they can move beyond getting work "done" and toward developing lifelong practices that serve them well as writers, communicators, and people.

Because one size can never fit all, we need knowledge and experience related to what and why people write, as well as understandings about possible options for how words and images are assembled on page and screen. Then we need to make intentional decisions to live our visions—we need to walk our talk.

Real Time, Real Life: Animating Understandings, Negotiating Practices, Making Decisions, and Supporting Writers

Decisions are made by people. The next chapters focus on decisions made by teachers and students alike. Because this book aims to illustrate how writers and teachers of writers bring their visions and beliefs to life through the decisions they make and practices they craft, it is important for you to know more intimately some of the classrooms and teachers that you'll meet in the coming pages. These teachers work in a variety of contexts and represent a range of experiences. Some spend their days in public city schools, others in parochial city schools, and others in suburban or small-town contexts. Some work with multilingual students, others with more culturally homogeneous groups. Some teach in places where nearly 100 percent of students receive free or reduced lunch, others in places with fewer economic challenges. Some have been graduate students of mine, others are colleagues from my early days of teaching, and still others are members of school faculties that I've met over the years as I've collaborated with their schools as a consultant, university partner, or teacher education faculty member. Some have traveled through traditional teacher education programs; others have gained certification through alternative routes. Their experiences in the field range from just beginning to teach to more than twenty years of experience. Some know each other personally; some know about each other because, through DVDs and stories told, they've been able to observe the writing practices in one anothers' classrooms. Despite the differences in their classroom contexts and pathways to and within education, they share a commitment to constant envisioning and revisioning the learning opportunities in their classrooms. They draw on resources—professional books, colleagues, published units of study, professional organizations, diverse professional development opportunities—and work to navigate the local challenges of their teaching contexts so they can own their instructional decisions. Even when a school or district curriculum directs aspects of their days, they still find ways to make decisions that they believe are suited to the students in their classrooms so that these writers become the writers they have envisioned. The following chapters draw from these teachers' classrooms and the thinking that informs the ongoing growth of young writers and writing instruction.

As you read the pages and cases to come, keep in mind that these teachers aren't the only ones making decisions. Common to each of their visions is the belief that students should be well aware of what they're doing in their writing and why. Teacher decisions are often linked to helping young people see and articulate what they are doing. So, in the cases to come, you'll find teachers discussing decisions they've made about how to create a structure and spaces in which their students become active participants in bringing these visions to life.

Making Decisions: Why We Write, What We Write, and How We Write

Writers, young and old, aren't the only ones charged with on-going decision making—their mentors, editors, and teachers also make decisions all the time. Teachers themselves must constantly make decisions about the best ways to help shape writers' thinking and decision-making skills related to how they write, why they write, and what they write as they live and participate in a diverse, constantly changing society.

Because preparing writers for rich and active social lives as engaged citizens is complex work, this chapter focuses on decisions that teachers and their students make in terms of the *whys*, *whats*, and *hows* of writing. I first look at *why* we write, and why we ask our students to write, and how our reasons for writing inform *what* it is that we compose and *what* it is that we do with the words on the page or screen. In other words, *why* and *what* we write are inter-related questions that get at purpose (both personal and social) and form. This focus on *why* and *what* speaks directly to the need to help young people understand what it means to be a writer, taking into consideration the many complexities and prior experiences associated with that role. For example, one time when I was a guest in a third-grade classroom conferring with students during a picture book publication process, one student told me that the reason he had little on his paper was that he was not going to *be a writer*; rather, he had clear plans to *become a veterinarian*. While I was initially taken aback by his comment, I soon realized that young writers like this boy need to know that veterinarians *do* write, as do bloggers, as do store clerks, as do grandparents, and so on. One only need browse the National Gallery of Writing (www.galleryofwriting.org) to find examples of diverse ways and reasons we compose. Sometimes writers write to tell stories of being home alone, sometimes to commemorate an occasion through poetry, or to engage in reflection about a particular moment in their lives. But writers also produce reports, convey research, write editorials, and communicate electronically. And, once they have a clear purpose, all writers, from book authors, to bloggers, to veterinarians, make decisions about *what* they will write—that is, the form their writing will take—as well as *how* they will write—that is, the processes that work best for them, the language(s) they use, and the techniques they employ.

This decision-making process is undoubtedly complicated for any writer, but it is an increasingly vital skill for young writers to recognize and practice. As I will argue in this chapter, this approach to teaching writing—seeing writing as a series of decisions made by the writer, and writing instruction as a series of decisions made by teachers—is complicated, especially if a teacher seeks to help a classroom full of young writers learn how to make decisions that will result in good writing and flexibility as writers. Decision making in the writing classroom, then, is about young writers and how they learn to make individual decisions in their writing, as well as about teachers and how they come to make decisions in their writing curriculum. And each and every decision we make or that young writers make circles back to our visions for writers, writing, and what it means to learn to write well.

To connect real students, teachers, and classrooms with the decision making that writers and their teachers engage with, I share cases in this chapter from real classes in which I have collaborated. The examples I share will, I hope, demonstrate for you the sometimes explicit and sometimes behind-the-scenes decisions that teachers make in the name of helping their students, and how those decisions link back to the visions these teachers bring to the classroom setting. As you read, I urge you to think about your own visions and the decisions you need to make on a daily basis.

Why and What: The Connections between Purpose and Form

What writers produce depends on circumstance and purpose, a point that is evident in our everyday lives as we read and write in a variety of ways for many

different purposes. Consider, for example, the kinds of writing involved with organizing a party. If you decide to write and send invitations, you have to think about
the particular features common to this genre since readers will need to know when
the party will occur, where it will be held, what time the celebration begins and
ends, and so on. Now think about another example of writing you might engage
in: weighing in on the need to improve the community recycling program. While
your purpose might initially be clear, you must make decisions about the genres
you might use to express your stance. You could, for example, send an email to
your alderman, write an op-ed for the newspaper, craft a petition for the neighborhood, and so on. What these two situations demonstrate is this: writers need to
understand that different types of writing have different purposes and thus forms.
Although at times writers may come to this understanding by studying a particular genre such as personal narrative or letter writing, they also need experience in
connecting their ideas and intentions with the forms that make best sense for their
purpose and audience. This line of thinking led two-upper elementary teachers to
combine their observations of their students with their belief that writing is intimately tied to purpose.

In early April, Katie and her fourth-grade students as well as Jacque and her
fifth-grade students were reading *Bud, Not Buddy* (Curtis, 1999). As they all read,
their conversations and writings became more and more intense. Students picked
up on the issue of racism, as illustrated in a "write-around" in their writing notebooks (see Figure 3.1 in the sidebar on page 30). In their class discussions, they
made connections between current life and the issues raised by Christopher Paul
Curtis. Students commented on how Curtis's writing made them think about important ideas and issues. As they read, talked, and wrote, students began to wonder
how their own writing could impact readers in the same way.

Up until April, these fourth and fifth graders and their teachers had collectively studied biographies, feature articles, wordless picture books, fiction, personal narratives, letter writing, fairy tales, and poetry. In their classrooms, they'd
engaged in lively conversations about politics, elections, health concerns, and
worldwide issues such as the H1N1 flu outbreak. Most of their writing, however,
remained anchored in their personal lives for an audience of their teacher and
classmates. Seeing students' interest in writing for broader audiences and purposes,
Katie and Jacque designed a unit of study called "World Writing," which they
and their students came to collectively define as writing about social issues such as
peace, war, love, segregation, moral lessons, historical events, people helping others, problems in the world, accepting differences, change, and so forth. While not
a conventional genre such as invitations, fantasy, or memoir, writing of this nature
was united by a common purpose. Teachers and students saw this kind of writing
as texts that spoke to issues of importance to the authors and to the world. They

set off to study together how writers made their thinking known and how writers invited others to think and act on behalf of these issues (see Figure 3.2).

As young writers, the students were passionate about different issues and wanted to educate others about issues that they cared deeply about, such as cancer, Relay for Life, animal protection, and the environment. The unit Katie and Jacque designed invited students to pursue projects about self-selected issues. *What* they would each publish would vary and be directly tied to *why* they were writing it. If their reason for writing spoke directly to a particular company and its decisions, a letter might be the genre of choice. If their intentions were broader, an article,

Write-Around

A *write-around* is a way to gather, in print, multiple people's thinking about a given topic or issue. While similar to a written conversation, a write-around generally includes more participants and allows multiple lines of thinking to be circulating simultaneously.

1. Each participant in a small group (or whole class) frames an initial statement or question that they hope to get a response to. The question and the author's name are clearly written at the top of a piece of paper.

2. Questions are passed one person to the right. Readers take time to read the initial question or issue and then record their thoughts on the topic. After a set period of time, papers are passed to the right again.

3. Readers take time to read the initial question or issue as well as the response(s) and then add their own. Exchanges continue until enough people have responded to generate a substantive "conversation," and papers are then returned to the initial author, who can then read classmates' thinking about the question or issue originally put forth.

Figure 3.1: Example of a student write-around.

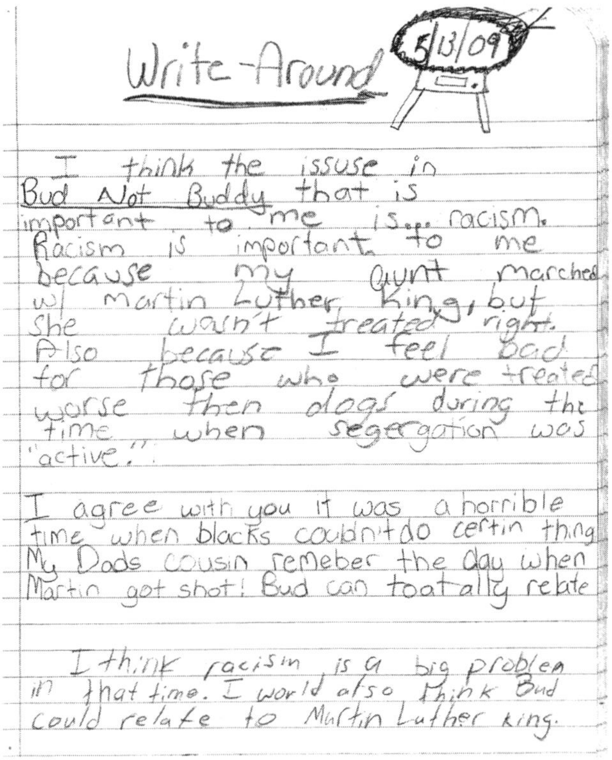

poem, or commentary might be best. Believing that form is intimately tied to purpose, Katie and Jacque supported their writers through lessons and conferences focused on the links between audience, purpose and form (see Figure 3.3).

Figure 3.2: What do we mean by world writing? A collection of student ideas.

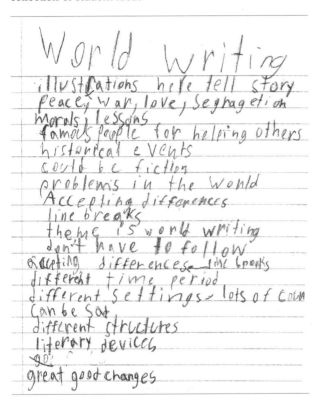

Figure 3.3: Form used for a mini-lesson: Matching genre with intended purpose.

Curricular statement (knowledge that informs and shapes teaching):
Writers make decisions about what genre would best suit their purpose for writing.

Lesson Procedure:
1. Connect with the writing work students have done to date, as well as with their recent reading lives. In this case, students have written in many forms and genres ranging from fairy tales and letters to biographies and personal narratives. Their teachers have intentionally invited students to read and explore (in readerly and writerly ways) an essay from *Newsweek* written by President Obama, a poem on social issues from Naomi Shihab Nye's *Honeybee*, an article from *Scholastic News*, and an editorial from the newspaper.

continued on next page

continued from previous page

2. Present students with a handout chart they can use as a note-taking device during the lesson. In the featured case, we distributed a PowerPoint slide that listed some of the genres studied to date and a two-column chart. In the first column, we listed writers' intentions for each of the pieces we had explored as a class—asking why someone might compose a piece and/or what they hope the writing accomplishes. The second column included a header "Possible genre (& example)."

Teach

Poetry - Essay - Opinion Piece - Feature Article - Story - Letter

Purpose of piece/Writers intention (what you hope your writing does)	Possible genre (& example)
Help reader think about _____ in a particular way	Feature Article. Letter, Essay
Encourage reader to ACT or do something	Opinion piece
Explain author's thinking	Story, Feature Article, Autobiography
Raise awareness	Essay, Artical, Poem.
Inform people about important event, person, or issue	Article, Opinion. Letter, Poetry
Explain opinion	Opinion piece. Article
Other: inspire people	Poetry Featured. Article Opinion Piece.
Other: Explain facts	Opinion Piece. Essay, Article

3. Invite students to think about their current writing agendas and interests (either from memory or by exploring past notebook entries). Have them take five or so minutes with a partner to consider what they want to accomplish with the writing project they're currently pursuing. With their goals in mind, they can brainstorm what genres they might use. Encourage students to generate multiple possibilities.
4. Ask students to briefly share some of their thinking and reasons why they feel particular genres could accomplish the purposes listed.
5. Remind students to use these notes to help them move from the researching and developing phases of writing into writing their drafts. They should begin to draft in a genre that best suits their purposes. Olene, for example, had interviewed friends and family about issues of inclusion, exclusion, and care. She began drafting a poem. When asked why, she explained that she thought a poem would make people stop to think and, as a writer, she saw poetry as a way to include direct quotes from her interviews as lines in her poem.
6. Highlight students' decisions. After providing adequate time for a good number of writers to begin drafts, ask students to share their current genre selection, their reasoning for picking the genre, and how their decision is working out (so far . . . keeping in mind that writers sometimes, or often, change their minds!).

Katie and Jacque's shared vision for writers includes the belief that what a person writes is tied to the purpose(s) the writer is pursuing. These teachers' thinking and actions in the classroom illustrate one set of options and decisions about why writers write and what and how they compose. But other visions and approaches are possible as well. The following cases highlight how other teachers enact their visions for young writers as they work to teach young people about what writers might compose and why. Each case begins with an introduction to the writer and his or her teacher, with attention given to the teacher's vision for writers. Each case then features a teaching and learning interaction, often including sample lessons, example conferences, or student work that illustrates a key point in the case, followed by a discussion of the case that focuses on the decisions that were made and the impact of those decisions on the student's life or identity as a writer. As you read each case, note the connections between the decisions made and the vision for writers. Consider other decisions the teacher and young writers have made and how they resonate with the stated vision. And think about how the visions shared and decisions made relate to you and your students' current visions and decision-making practices.

> **Why Writers Write and What They Write: Highlighting Featured Cases**
>
> - Writers remember and writers record: Putting life experiences into print.
>
> - Writers report: Moving beyond writing as personal stories and make-believe.
>
> - Writers react: Reading, questioning, and responding.
>
> - Writers communicate: Using own and others' perspectives to share thinking and learning.
>
> - Writers anticipate and seek response: Joining virtual writing communities.
>
> - Writers change minds: Inviting readers to consider other perspectives.

Writers Remember and Writers Record: Putting Life Experiences into Print

Meet sixth grader Arcelia, third grader Antonio, and kindergartner Juan. They are all writers with full lives. They spend their days in different classrooms in a public school committed to fostering their growth as writers from their preK years to eighth grade and beyond. Their teachers believe that "writing is more meaningful for students when they can choose what they write about" and that they need to create "classrooms that, more than anything, give students a voice." They also believe that becoming a writer is "an ever-changing and evolving process [through which s]tudents develop at their own pace." Each of their teachers strives to create a classroom in which time is regularly dedicated to writing and is accompanied by intentional teaching that supports writers' growth. Their teachers began the year inviting students to compose personal narratives, believing that beginning the year in-the-known (i.e., with students' life experiences) might best support success and build the communities needed to support writers across the year.

Using their lives as a resource, the students wrote about family events, significant moments in their school lives, as well as their dreams and goals (see Figure 3.4). *What* they wrote—narratives—was similar from child to child even though

Figure 3.4: Students narrated their memories and their lives.

Juan: In the Park

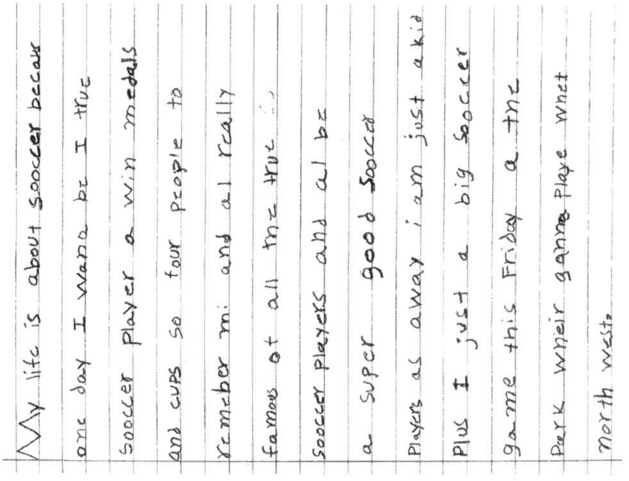

Antonio: Soccer Life

My life is about soccer becaus

one day I wanna be I true

soccer player a win medals

and cups so tour people to

remeber mi and al really

famous ot all the true

soccer players and al be

a super good soccer

players as away i am just a kid

Plus I just a big soccer

game this Friday a the

Park wheir gonna playe what

north west.

Arcelia: Homework Trouble

Trouble!

Parent signature Screamed

the teacher, Why dint you do your

homework becouse I

dont tell me, while it in a sheet

of paper, It was 3:00 o'clock. When

the teacher was collecting the ho-

mework And I was the ony one who

dint dit her homework, So I hadted

to stay after school half hour to clean

up the hole from All of the

girls were staring at me

And also laughing I feel like

punching them, I feel bad that

they were killing my role

classmates. I hate does girls

there were to gustD

And frankly the pricipal

saw them and they saw

they hadted to help me. That

when I dicided to

alwous do my home-

work. Eventh the half hour

was gooe And I got out of

the school. I feel like I was

in Jail. And I've gyto girls hatted

so show longer then me.

some wrote only with pictures, others with pictures and text, and others with English and/or Spanish text. But *why* they wrote varied. Arcelia wrote about a time when her homework wasn't done, because this was a time she remembered well and wanted to avoid in the future. When reflecting on the piece and her reasons for writing, she commented that she could hear the teacher's voice, remember the humiliation of being interrupted, and easily recall the thoughts going through her mind as she attempted to respond to the teacher and deal with peers. Antonio wrote his piece because, according to him, "soccer is my life," while his classmate wrote about a recent visit to 26th Street, using its Spanish name, *viente seis*, because she recognized that the language used reflected the essence of the place. And Juan wrote to capture a recent day-in-the-park experience. As these students put their lives on paper using narration, dialogue, image, and multiple languages, they not only recorded memories but also came to see their experiences as significant. They wrote these pieces early in the year as part of new classroom and school communities. Their writing not only demonstrated what they knew as writers, but it also created windows into their lives, allowing their readers to learn about them as people.

In this scenario, the teachers and students made numerous decisions, including:

- Teachers decided that putting students' lives first would build community while providing critical information about each of their student's skills and experiences as writers at the beginning of the year, a decision that reflected their visions of the classrooms they hoped to create.

- Arcelia decided that writing about a memorable moment would help her compose a realistic piece because she had lived the details.

- Antonio and other members of his class decided that collections of memories (such as those based on being an avid soccer fan and player) could lead a writer from memories to goals and aspirations, and that the language used could help capture both place and experience.

- Juan decided that detailed images could capture and communicate his thinking.

But while writing from lived experience is motivating for some, it does not move all writers to write. As I illustrate in the next section, some writers have different motivations and therefore what they choose to write varies in form and function.

Writers Report: Moving beyond Writing as Personal Stories and Make-Believe

Meet Milo. He's an energetic second grader who has recently immigrated to the United States from Bosnia. During reading time, he is often poring over nonfiction, studying the details of how things work, finding locations mentioned in texts on a nearby map, or reading recipes (including those at the back of nonfiction books about various countries) and scheming about how he might secure the ingredients to try cooking such items at home. Although a voracious reader, Milo describes his feelings about writing in these early days in second grade with Kellie as his teacher: "I'm not a writer. I'm a reader." And his actions matched his words; his new writing notebook was one of the few in the classroom with empty pages; they stared back at him and his teacher each time the cover was cracked. Kellie longed to help Milo put his thinking to paper. As a teacher of young writers, Kellie saw reading and writing as related enterprises and knew writers needed access to multiple writing modalities. Therefore, she invited the kids in her classroom to write about anything in the ways and language(s) they felt most comfortable. Despite these open invitations, when it came time to write, Milo read. Milo's notebook remained unused.

During a conference, Milo revealed that he didn't like to imagine things; he preferred things that were real, like newspaper articles. This provided Kellie with two important insights: one, that Milo associated writing with personal stories and fiction and, two, that he was interested in the newspaper. When Kellie asked if he read newspapers or knew about people who wrote articles for newspapers, Milo seemed to know little but was highly interested. Soon Kellie started bringing a copy of the *Chicago Tribune* to school, and Milo started his days by reading the paper and writing about what he'd read and thought (see Figure 3.5).

In this case, Kellie made visible to this young person the idea that writers are readers too, and that writers often use their reading to launch into written lines of thinking. The teaching she offered grew out of a conference interaction, but the introduction of the newspaper in the classroom and the writing practices that developed as Milo and his classmates read and responded to articles were evident in the following days, weeks, and months. These activities challenged the myth that writers are people who craft only fiction and tell imaginary stories; they also allowed Milo and his classmates to explicitly experience how writers make use of tools (in this case a newspaper) to aid in their writing processes and practices. The most obvious impact of this teaching was that Milo began to write—about museum exhibits, about war, about John F. Kennedy, and about being a collector of foreign currency. Over time, he began to see himself not only as a reporter but also as a writer more generally. He came to believe this not because he was told so, but because he could see the fruits and fluency of his work as it gradually became "easy" to put ideas on the page.

To get Milo to this point, he and his teacher made a number of decisions:

- Milo's teacher decided to listen to young writers with attention and intention.
- Milo's teacher decided to bring resources into the classroom to match her students' interests and inquiries.

Figure 3.5: Writing to report: Milo writes about the science museum in the news.

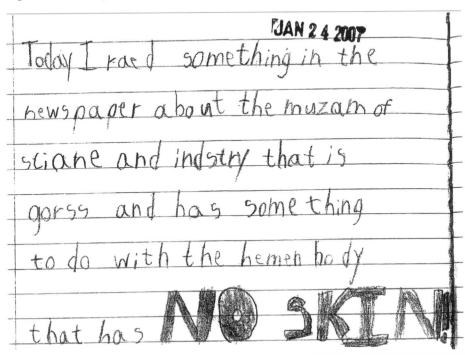

- Milo decided that writing could be more than personal storytelling.
- Milo decided that reporting what he read was a form of writing that suited his purposes.

While some writers are inspired to write by reporting on issues as they unfold, using published pieces as models and mentor texts, others are inspired by reading, questioning, and responding to a variety of texts, as you will see in the next example.

Writers React: Reading, Questioning, and Responding

Meet Claudia. Her notebook is filled with stories of family travels, cupcakes, snow in April, and the recent adoption of a new little sister. She is a fourth-grade writer who seems to select personal topics with ease. Katie, her teacher, believes that reading and writing practices are intertwined and that writing is a tool for thinking. She also believes that writers need to see a wide range of purposes for writing. To further develop students' writing repertoires to include experiences with writing as a tool for questioning and reacting to the surrounding social world, Katie had Claudia and her classmates participate in a mini-lesson that focused on the ways in which writers respond to others' written work (see Figure 3.6).

Figure 3.6: Mini-lesson: Using notebooks as a space to react.

Background and Purpose

Teachers who carefully study student notebook writing can detect patterns and thus help nudge students into new ways of writing. In this case, teachers had observed that students' notebook writing was anchored in personal stories, whereas students' talk and ways of interacting with the world went beyond personal storytelling and reflection.

Curricular Statement (knowledge that informs and shapes teaching)

Writers use their notebooks as a thinking space, as a place to react and shape response to issues and happenings alive in the world.

Materials Needed

Student notebooks, newspapers, newsmagazines, Internet printouts of recent news, chart paper, markers, scissors, glue stick or tape

Lesson Procedure

1. Share the purpose of the lesson by telling students that today they are going to explore how writers can use their notebooks to react to issues and events—and that writing can help them discover what they think. In other words, firm opinions need not exist before writers start to write.
2. Demonstrate how a person might go about reacting to world, community, or school issues by first noting that to react to what's going on, you need to have a sense of current happenings. Rather than simply trying to remember or "think of" issues, print media can help us select topics and issues to react to. To show students how they might do this, select an article, cut or print it out, place it on a clean notebook page, read it, and begin to react on paper *as* you read. Write margin notes, circle parts that strike you, or use the questions below to prompt further thinking.
3. Offer a list of critical questions for readers to consider while reading. (Asking students to *react* can prompt not only a shift in writing but also a shift in reading and thinking.) Possible questions could include:

   - What is the tone of the piece?
   - What perspective did the author take?
   - What form of writing is this? Why might the author have selected this form?
   - Why did I pick this piece?
   - After reading the piece, what was I thinking?
   - Did I like or dislike what I read? What made me like or dislike the piece?
   - What might I have done differently?
   - What did the author do that I might use next time I write?

4. Demonstrate how you might react—underline, draw lines from the printed text to the notebook margin, and add comments, questions, or thoughts.
5. Invite kids to select from reading materials supplied and try the same process.
6. Share examples of what students tried during independent writing time and angle conversation toward where and when in their everyday lives they might find or select issues to react to in the future.

Responding to the mini-lesson, Claudia dove into reading, writing, and reacting. She began by clipping an article about the recent release of Amazon's latest edition of the Kindle. She used the mini-lesson questions as a guide, but rather than responding to every question, she selected those that "fit best" and that made the most sense to her given the article she'd selected. Claudia began with suggestions for how the author might have approached the writing of this piece differently. She then generated information left out of the piece and provided her own commentary on the relationship between the expense of the Kindle and who may or may not have access to this tool (see Figure 3.7). The Kindle entry was not the only time Claudia used these reading, questioning, and responding practices in her writing life. Subsequent entries in her notebook included articles with her commentary. For example, while reading a *Sun Times* article about a dog owner who jumped in Lake Michigan to rescue his dog, Claudia not only commented on the owner's actions but also, within the text of the clipped article, underlined the words *dissuade* and *plucked*, noting that she liked the language selected.

Katie offered Claudia and her classmates a set of reading practices that had the potential to impact the ways in which they engaged with writing. The mini-lesson provided a menu of questions, and writing time and tools allowed writers to try their hand at responding to another writer's work. This set of practices moved Claudia, and many of her classmates, into new writing practices that stretched the definitions and possibilities for using writing in their lives. They moved beyond describing what was happening in the world to reacting, offering their perspectives and learning to take a stand. While this teaching did expand the topics students wrote about, to Katie the intention was about more than expanding topics—it was about taking on a new stance as a writer and a person.

Although Claudia was using her writing to think and question, her writing was a private piece tucked inside her notebook. However, she may, at a later date, return to this entry and share it with others, or draw on the thinking practices in a new context.

Helping Claudia understand how to use reading, questioning, and responding to become a better writer required a number of decisions on both Claudia's and her teacher's parts:

- Claudia's teacher decided to expand the ways in which her students were using writing to move them beyond personal writing to include critical reflection.
- Claudia decided to sort through the provided questions to select those that best fit her article and interests.
- Claudia decided to draw on her own knowledge about the work of writers to identify interesting words for potential future use.

Figure 3.7: Writing to react: Claudia's response to an article on the Kindle.

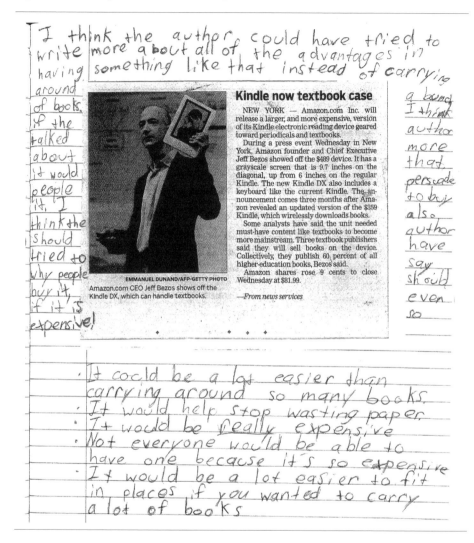

I think the author could have tried to write more about all of the advantages in having something like that instead of carrying around of books. If they talked about it would people it, I think they should tried to why people buy it, if it is expensive!

a bund I think author more that persade to buy also author have say should even so

Kindle now textbook case

NEW YORK — Amazon.com Inc. will release a larger, and more expensive, version of its Kindle electronic reading device geared toward periodicals and textbooks.

During a press event Wednesday in New York, Amazon founder and Chief Executive Jeff Bezos showed off the $489 device. It has a grayscale screen that is 9.7 inches on the diagonal, up from 6 inches on the regular Kindle. The new Kindle DX also includes a keyboard like the current Kindle. The announcement comes three months after Amazon revealed an updated version of the $359 Kindle, which wirelessly downloads books.

Some analysts have said the unit needed must-have content like textbooks to become more mainstream. Three textbook publishers said they will sell books on the device. Collectively, they publish 60 percent of all higher-education books, Bezos said.

Amazon shares rose 9 cents to close Wednesday at $81.99.

—From news services

EMMANUEL DUNAND/AFP-GETTY PHOTO
Amazon.com CEO Jeff Bezos shows off the Kindle DX, which can handle textbooks.

- It could be a lot easier than carrying around so many books.
- It would help stop wasting paper.
- It would be really expensive
- Not everyone would be able to have one because it's so expensive
- It would be a lot easier to fit in places if you wanted to carry a lot of books

- Claudia decided to carry a strategy from one mini-lesson forward into future reading and writing work.

Using published texts to encourage students to engage in new ideas is one way to inspire different approaches to writing. Another way, illustrated in the next classroom scenario, is to encourage young writers to listen to others' perspectives in order to increase their understanding and then communicate the shared thinking with expanded audiences.

Writers Communicate: Using Own and Others' Perspectives to Share Thinking and Learning

Meet second-grade writers from Room 202. These second graders live in a classroom where their teacher longs for the students to enjoy writing and to see the range of ways in which writers use written words. Their teacher, Aimee, believes that to write well, students must have experience writing often and for purposes of their own (and at times others') choosing. Aimee constantly reflects on teaching and revises her curriculum as she works to best match students' needs with instruction. Initially, she provided students with notebooks in which they could collect their thinking about issues and events on their minds, personally reflect on these issues and events, and return to as a resource when working on to-be-published pieces. As the year progressed, Aimee thought more about the role of reflection in students' learning processes, as well as the role of audience—specifically, the importance of writing for readers beyond their classroom. She and the students created the "Second Grade Scoop" newsletter, to which class members were invited to submit monthly stories about their learning, school events, and important moments.

While students' notebooks began to fill with personal reflections in the form of letters to their parents; thoughts on what it was like to be seven (right after one writer had turned eight); first tastes of new foods; and passions for particular books, movies, and video games, the students' newsletter articles engaged these writers in a different sort of reflection and thinking on paper. In their articles, the students reflected on school happenings, from both their perspectives and others', as they consulted with others during their writing processes (see Figure 3.8).

The process of putting their thinking about class experiences into print helped these young people clarify their own thinking while considering how other people's thinking fit with the experiences they were trying to capture in print. As these writers looked back on experiences, gathered peer perspectives, and composed for a genuine, beyond-the-classroom audience, they were constantly making decisions.

To create a published newsletter, the students and their teacher made a number of decisions:

- The second graders' teacher decided that a newsletter forum could move students beyond personal reflections and provide opportunities to explore new communicative purposes and forms of writing.
- Julián and John decided that including specific events from a book and specific parts of a map were important for readers to best understand the classroom experiences they were trying to animate in their writing.

Figure 3.8: Writing to communicate: The "Second Grade Scoop" newsletter.

Maps

by Julian

We learned about maps in October. We made maps in October. Wade thinks they are cool and Olene does too. Some maps look like places and others look like continents. Maps have compass roses and map keys. We learned a lot about maps.

Rocket Run

By Wade

"We are ready to go to the rocket run," I said, "Are you ready Ethan?"…When Mr. R blows the whistle, rocket run will begin. He blew the whistle. I started running. 28 minutes later, then he said 2 minutes left. Then 30 more seconds of rocket run. 29, 28, 27, 26, 25, 24, ….4, 3, 2, 1. … At the end of the day at school they reported 2 people who won their class. Ms. I said Wade and Ethan were the winners. Wade ran 35 laps and Ethan ran 34. On Monday morning meeting, me and Ethan got medals. Maybe you could win a medal too.

Clementine

By John

Guess what my class is reading? We are reading Clementine! It is a very good book. It's about girl who keeps doing CRAZY things!

When you are in second grade, you'll read at least two. "I think Clementine is funny and I really like the book stated Lucas. "I like Clementine because of the pigeon wars," sputtered Ethan. My favorite part was when she told her teacher she was moving to Egypt, said John. My class thinks Clementine is a good book.

Dr. Katie

By Olene

Dr. Katie, when she came in the classroom, the class so excited. Catarina said she said we were smart writers. Greg said, "he liked the video." I liked when she wrote the list. Kailey said she liked when she told us about writing….Niles said she liked being with smart writers.

- Wade decided that including the countdown of seconds would make readers feel like they were on the scene watching the runners.

- Olene decided that including many perspectives was important, since the whole class was there when I (Dr. Katie) visited.

Using writing as a tool for communication can help writers learn new ways to share their thoughts with specific audiences, moving beyond their own thoughts to gather additional information from others. Furthering this approach to writing, the next case features writers for whom response from readers is intimately tied to their purpose and actions.

Writers Anticipate and Seek Response: Joining Virtual Writing Communities

As upper-elementary students, Sabina and Devin write with readers' responses at the forefront of their minds. Although in this case their intentions are similar, their histories vary. Sabina, currently in the sixth grade in Chicago, has been an avid reader and writer for most of her life. At only twelve years old, she is an aunt (something she writes about regularly) and lives in a home where multiple languages are spoken on a regular basis. Having read many of her notebook entries over the years, I was intrigued when she mentioned she was blogging. Over the summer, her new middle-grades teachers launched middle school blogs for students. Upon invitation, Sabina was the first of the new bloggers to respond ("Thank you can't wait till August to start bloging about the book :)") and was the only one to include a picture of herself. As she and her classmates launched into a discussion of Paul Fleischman's book *Seedfolks* (2004), Sabina again was the first to respond, noting:

> i notice that there were a lot of prob.
>
> 1-the garden is really messy.P.3
>
> 2-it's dangerous to enter to the garden.p.9
>
> 3-a lot of people r interested in this garden.(no page # i notice this)
>
> 4-people r willing to help fix this garden.p.12,16

When reflecting on blogging, Sabina noted the differences in this communication venue: "[I]n blog writing you don't have to stick to one thing or one topic. . . . In regular writing you don't usually get responses. People won't really go into your [regular] writing and say I disagree with you because . . . , but when you're writing a blog it's more like 'I'll write this so they won't disagree' or 'I wonder what people would think about . . .' and so you write something and find out." Sabina was doing more than completing an assignment. While she was learning to use new technologies and to communicate in multiple modalities, she also was learning about rhetorical moves that would cause readers and responders to engage with her thinking in particular ways. She was learning that becoming a writer is about engaging and thinking with others.

Whereas Sabina knew response was an integral part of blogging, Devin saw response as a motivation to write. Devin, a fourth grader who often struggles to stay organized and finish work, demonstrated the power of response in a different way. Fourth- and fifth-grade students in his school had been invited by the school literacy coach to read George Ella Lyon's poem "Where I'm From" (1999), make lists of what matters in their lives (Christensen, 2000), and eventually compose poems about their lives to submit to the National Gallery of Writing (http://www.galleryofwriting.org/). At the same time, community college students in a neighboring state had been invited to compose and submit poetry as well. Initially, Devin did not express interest in writing a poem of his own. When the National Day on Writing arrived and people began reading the submissions in the gallery, his literacy coach shared an email response she'd received from college writers about the poems submitted by the fourth and fifth graders. This response piqued Devin's interest. "I want to be in that thing. I want to be like those college kids," he told his literacy coach. Later that day, during math, Devin's teacher found him focused on writing and commented that Devin had told her that he "needed to work on something" and therefore needed the time to write. Devin finished his poem and uploaded his piece into the gallery. As he marveled at seeing his own piece alongside others, Devin noted, "I could do more of that." For Devin, writing the "Where I'm From" poem was not about completing an assignment—that was optional. It was about contributing to an interactive space where he could see his work alongside others and could receive feedback from those he admired. With his piece in the gallery, he was a successful writer, ready to "do more."

To help Devin, Sabina, and their classmates see writing as a way to communicate with others, their teachers made a number of decisions, and the children made some decisions too:

- Sabina's teacher decided to use technology as a means of communication, understanding the shifts in conventions and discourse associated with the genre of blogs.
- Sabina decided that blogs call for different language conventions.
- Sabina decided that what she wrote was influenced by potential reader response—when writing in a dialogic forum, what one says and how one crafts a message are influenced by possible responses.
- Devin's literacy coach decided to unite diverse communities of writers to provide real windows into what it means to be an elementary or a college writer.
- Devin decided to write, revise, and publish—driven by response.
- Devin's teacher decided that Devin needed to use math time to express stamina and commitment to a clear purpose.

Writing for public audiences and receiving feedback from those audiences clearly inspires some writers to make their voices heard. For others, it's all about finding a passion, especially if that passion has to do with changing someone else's mind, something you will see illustrated in the next vignette.

Writers Change Minds: Inviting Readers to Consider Other Perspectives

Meet Jeremy, a writer who lived in a fourth-grade classroom where his teacher wanted her students to move beyond merely naming "entertain," "inform," or "persuade" as the purpose for writing in order to experience what it means to use writing to shape or reshape readers' thinking. This meant that young writers like Jeremy needed passion for their work, a clear sense of purpose, and a sense of what their audience believes or thinks so that they can organize content to meet their goals.

Jeremy wasn't just a writer; he was a sports fan. Sports talk was commonplace amongst his friends and classmates. Jeremy very much enjoyed these conversations and drew on them in his writing as well, reflecting on Favre's future or exploring his thinking on recent suspensions of athletes. In the spring, as the Cubs called up a player named Bobby Scales from the minors, talk turned to the failures and mistakes made by the new Chicago Cub. Jeremy saw it differently, and he wanted others to see the player as someone who persevered and kept going even when times were tough. So Jeremy began to draft an article. Keeping classmate comments in mind, he combined what he knew about Bobby Scales with interviews and background information he'd found online. Wanting his readers to walk away seeing Scales as someone who "never gives up and keeps on trying," Jeremy decided to write a piece that would show Scales's efforts (see Figure 3.9). He also decided to include more than his own opinion. Jeremy found a quote from one of Scales's teammates that illustrated the team's support for the new player's stamina as they hugged him after his first major league hit and for his first major league strikeout.

Jeremy had a clear sense of purpose when composing this piece because conversations in his own life drove him to compose. He had recorded his purpose in his writer's notebook as part of his drafting process, and he reread and revised his draft with his purpose in mind, specifically stating his purpose in his fifth paragraph and again in his conclusion. As Jeremy wrote, his teacher helped him learn new ways to achieve his purpose, which for Jeremy included infusing research findings into his writing. When his article was complete, the real test of Jeremy's success was his readers' reactions.

Jeremy learned in a classroom where writing was used for a variety of purposes and where teaching supported the students' own agendas. His teacher's vision was put in action as she taught Jeremy, along with several of his classmates with similar needs, how to locate useful resources and how to incorporate that research into their writing so that they could not only name reasons for writing, such as inform, entertain, persuade, or, in Jeremy's words, "inspire other readers," but also develop writing practices that allowed them to intentionally achieve their goals.

The decisions that Jeremy and his teacher made to help this happen included the following:

- Jeremy's teacher decided to connect Jeremy's passion for sports with his development as a writer.

Figure 3.9: Writing to change readers' minds: Jeremy lays out the case of Bobby Scales.

Eleven years and 3,303 minor league at bats. Would you give up or quit? Well Bobby Scales did not give up or quit! He had doubts about his career choice of playing baseball, but one day Big Z (Carlos Zambrano) got put on a day DL (Disabled List). The game came and Bobby Scales was facing The Freak Tim Lincicum; well Tim Lincicum couldn't stop Bobby from getting his first hit!

The pitch was a high fastball. Bobby got on the top of the ball. The ball found some open grass in left field. Right before Bobby stepped into the batters box there was no stats about his major league career because it was his first time batting.

When Scales came around and scored, Bobby walked to the dug out. He felt relief that he finally got his first hit and run. When he got into the dug out, hugs and congrats from his teammates was all he felt and heard.

The Buzz of Bobby Scales continues. After so long people told him "you're hanging on too long." But Bobby said "I never saw it as hanging on, that's the thing I always said (if I) go to the point where I felt like I wasn't getting any better. Where I was getting beat up and overmatched and dominated or embarrassed, I would stop playing, and I just never felt that way."

Bobby has gone through a lot in his career. He has been traded and dropped, but still never gave up his dream of becoming a professional baseball player. If I were Bobby I would get tired of playing in the minors for so long with the same routine. What if he gets dropped or traded and sent back to the minors? "I'm playing now and that's all I can worry about. There are so many things in the game of baseball you can worry about, but there are so many things you can't control."

After the game Cubs coach Lou Pinella said "Congratulations on his first major league hit, hopefully there's a lot more where that came from!!!" Cubs player Micah Hoffpauir said "I gave him a big hug after his first hit and told him to get that one out of the way. I also gave him a big hug after his first strikeout and I also said to get that one out of the way too! He's put in the time and worked hard he deserves everything he's got!!!

Bobby Scales has shown America to never give up. I say Congrats to Bobby because he deserved it. Bobby has shown the world to never quit or give up your dream. So be like Bobby and don't give up you're dream keep on trying. It might take a long, long, really long time, but if you try hard enough you will SUCCEED!!!!!!!!!

Quotes from ChicagoTribune.com

- Jeremy's teacher decided to expand the students' understandings of the reasons (purposes) writers write, and how they might achieve their purposes through diverse genres.
- Jeremy decided to use writing as a tool to shift readers' thinking.
- Jeremy decided to draw on other published resources in developing his piece.

All of these cases illustrate *why* young people engage with writing and the world, as well as highlight a diverse range of products that emerge given their various purposes for writing. Whether blogging, writing poetry, or crafting feature articles or notebook entries, writers and their teachers drew on their understandings about purpose and possible forms or forums for their writing. They also used tools and techniques that helped them discover, articulate, compose, revise, edit, and share their work.

The next collection of cases highlights the tools, techniques, and conditions that support writers in developing a wide repertoire of practices to draw on to help them achieve their purposes and intentions. Examining *how* writers compose can further help teachers of writers, as well as writers themselves, develop or envision writing processes and practices that work—for them.

How Writers Write: Possible Tools, Techniques, Practices, and Conditions for Writing Well

There is no one way to write well. There is not one process or set of steps that will work for everyone, all the time. Writing is an act of problem solving in which the writer learns to see the problems as well as find the tools and motivation to try them out in an attempt to find a solution. Each writer's process, while unique, shares common practices and draws on shared tools and techniques. Differences tend to lie in how each writer orchestrates his or her use of particular tools to get the work done. For example, I find the blank page or screen daunting. Years ago I figured out that if I cut and paste an old paragraph, sentence, or page of text from a previous piece onto a clean page or empty screen, it's much easier to get started. Time has taught me that even though I've often deleted the "old text" by the time a new product is ready for publication, with this strategy I can avoid the long stares into the screen hoping that something will come to me. A writing mentor also taught me that when I'm just about done writing on a particular day, instead of leaving off with the last paragraph of a section or last sentence in a paragraph, I should take a few more minutes to write the first words of the next paragraph or section, a practice that had served my mentor well in his writing life. At his sugges-tion, I tried it and it worked for me. This practice is now a regular part of my writ-

How Writers Write: Highlighting Featured Cases

- Writers require time: Making time for writing.

- Writers take responsibility: Knowing what to do, when, and why.

- Writers draw on their knowledge of language(s): Using multiple languages when writing.

- Writers use models: Using other writing to assist in composing.

- Writers revise: Learning and practicing revision tools.

- Writers guide readers: Using punctuation to control readings.

ing process and allows me to continue my writing projects across days, weeks, and months.

Just as I've figured out what works for me, all writers need to discover what works for them. This means we need to invite writers to try out a range of strategies, attend to what works for them and what doesn't, and come to know the set of tools and practices that works best for them. Therefore, our job as teachers of writers is to use our overall vision of who we want our writers to become as a way to inform our teaching decisions regarding possible practices students might find helpful in their writing lives. We also must help young people understand and use what works best for them. As you read the following cases, focus on the decisions made about the conditions, practices, tools, or techniques offered and used. Note how the young people talk and think strategically about their work. Chapter 4 will focus more on how we help other writers become more aware of the decisions they make. But for now, just attend to the range of decisions made.

Writers Require Time: Making Time for Writing

When we talk about becoming writers who write well, a common need is time, preferably uninterrupted time. The question or challenge of time is especially problematic in schools. Meet Aubry and Natalie. Both are teachers, Aubrey in her fourth year of teaching kindergartners and Natalie a more experienced teacher currently working with middle-grade students. At the beginning of the school year, both engaged in the familiar teacher task of creating their schedules. Both believed strongly in regular, sustained opportunities for their students to engage with writing and experience coherent writing instruction. At the same time, both encountered challenges—half-days with kindergartners, specials (release time for art, music, phys ed, etc.), other subject area curricula, other team member needs, and so forth. Holding tight to their beliefs and visions, both teachers engaged in "scheduling conferences"—conversations with colleagues, including me—to talk through possibilities that might help the results of the decisions they made to match their visions.

Aubrey decided to hold a structured writing workshop three times a week, on the days her students did not go to specials. She also made explicit her think-

Figure 3.10: Making room for writing: Scheduling writing times.

AM: MONDAY SCHEDULE 5/3/10
SHARED READING *HANDPRINTS*
WORD WORK ING WORD FAMILY
STATIONS **&** **GUIDED READING** 1. SCIENCE – GUPPY DIAGRAM 2. MATH – DICE ADDITION GAME 3. READER RESPONSE – ABC BOOK CENTER 4. GAMES & PUZZLES 5. INDEPENDENT READING GUIDED READING: FROGS & FISH
WRITING NON-FICTION WRITING ML: FINDING TOPICS
MATH STANDARD AND NON-STANDARD FEET MEASUREMENT MATH MEASUREMENT STORIES
SCIENCE VENN DIAGRAM OF GUPPIES AND GOLDFISH
READ ALOUD NON-FICTION READ ALOUD: ZOO ANIMALS

ing about the other times when students would be writing on a daily basis (see Figure 3.10). Centers in her classroom would always involve at least one literacy station—specifically, a reader-response station where children could use writing to respond to recent reading. While in many ways this type of writing gets at reading comprehension, it also asks writers to use their composing skills for a different purpose. Aubrey also established a writing center as a permanent feature of her classroom environment, a place where students could access materials and tools for writing notes, telling a story, making a list, etc. Finally, her approach to science learning included frequent recording of observations, predictions, and so on. This too was writing time, a time in which writing instruction could unfold as she and her students worked together.

Although Natalie held beliefs and visions for her middle-grade writers similar to those of Aubrey, the decisions she made were different. Natalie worked on a team that was somewhat departmentalized. The school schedule was designed so that she would meet with students daily for two short reading and writing blocks. Committed to long stretches of time for students' deep engagement with reading and writing work, Natalie decided to integrate her reading and writing time, focusing intentionally on aspects of writing at least two days each week, reading at least two days, and being responsive to students' needs on the fifth day. As far as Natalie is concerned, this is still not enough time, and so she continues to lobby for more and sees herself working with master schedule planning for the next year to create richer and deeper learning for her students.

Figuring out how to make time for writing requires some intentional decision making. Aubrey and Natalie made the following decisions:

- Aubrey decided to make time by intentionally weaving writing and writing instruction throughout the curriculum.
- Natalie decided to set aside days specifically for writing, and then days specifically for reading, so that students would have long stretches of time to engage in writing work.
- Natalie decided to advocate for revisions in the school master schedule to support desired learning outcomes.

Once time has been made for writing, writers must know what to do, when, and why: in other words, they need plans, and they need to be invested as well as supported as they pursue their plans, something I take up in the next section.

Writers Take Responsibility: Knowing What to Do, When, and Why

Meet Aimee. It's her first year of teaching. Aimee is a teacher who is steeped in a culture of reading and thinking about workshops and process orientations toward writing. She had an immediate vision for her students to become articulate, independent writers who spend the year with her as productive members of a second-grade learning community, as well as a long-term vision that they will move through school and life as passionate and strategic writers. The little people in her room were energetic. They craved one-on-one direction and support from their teacher. And in the first few weeks of school, they took to reading with responsibility and interest but resisted engagement in productive independent writing time.

As a reflective, committed teacher, Aimee stepped back to watch the students pursue their own agendas, which didn't relate to writing. Then she made some decisions in the hopes of reworking the activity she saw unfolding in her classroom.

She knew that writers learn to write by writing, which meant her students needed time, but she realized they also needed plans so that they could use that time well. This meant they needed to understand productive writing processes and practices, as well as have time to develop and determine what worked best for them.

Initially, Aimee had scheduled forty-minute to one-hour blocks for writing, but her first decision was to temporarily shrink that time in order to support student success. She taught mini-lessons focused on developing individual plans for writing time, and she and her class talked about the value of "sticking with" their work over time. She created stamina charts to reflect the amount of time students could successfully engage in independent writing work and independent reading work (see Figure 3.11). These charts allowed both Aimee and the students to see significant discrepancies in student engagement, so together they could think about possible reasons why the same group of kids could engage so well as readers yet struggle to use writing time well.

When first introducing the stamina charts, which would graph the amount of time the class as a whole could engage in productive writing work, Aimee made several other related decisions. First, she decided that she and her students would need to clearly articulate responsibilities or jobs during writing workshop—both teacher and student jobs. Initially, her job would be to observe writers and how

Figure 3.11: Charting growth in independent reading and writing over time.

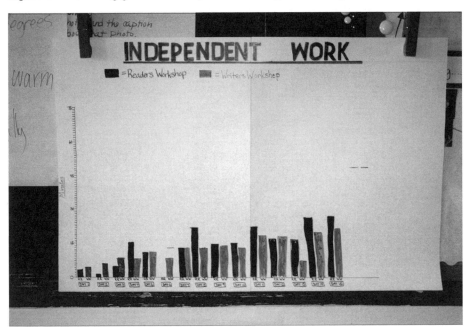

they engaged in writing work. This meant that she would not confer with writers, because she wanted to move students away from constant dependence on her. Second, she knew that some students struggled to settle into writing on their own. Because stamina charts would record whole-group activity, she decided to draw from her success with writing personalized notes to students in their reading logs and write notes to several writers in her class who she knew struggled to get started on their own. So, for instance, when Emma and Paul moved to their tables to write, they found notes from Aimee with questions related to their lives that were intended to help them begin writing "on their own" (see Figure 3.12). True, Aimee was still scaffolding their starts, but she was moving away from the daily one-to-one conferences previously required for these two writers. Last, Aimee decided that her teaching would need to focus on developing plans and writing agendas so that students wouldn't march through linear, prescribed writing processes but instead develop an awareness of what worked for them as individual writers working in a writing community.

In this case, the teacher wanted young writers to have an agenda and know why they were doing what they were doing. Valuing process means helping kids

Figure 3.12: Scaffolding starts: Aimee's notes to the writers.

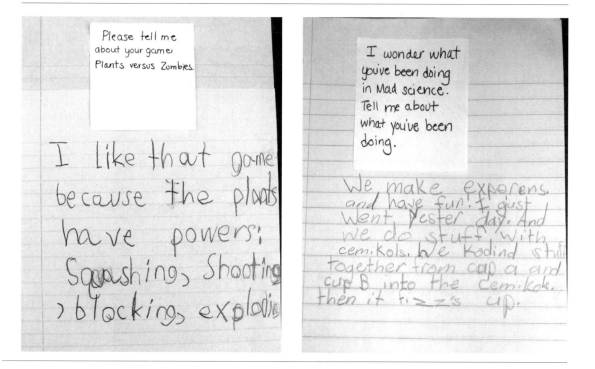

understand possible practices and how particular choices result in different destinations. As a reflective educator, Aimee stepped back to rethink her beliefs and had a go at realigning her practice to mirror her vision for writers. A number of decisions that she and her students made along the way helped the students take more responsibility for their writing:

- Aimee decided to take initial ownership of student practices by rethinking how writers could approach their practice in more productive ways.
- Aimee decided to temporarily adjust the schedule to facilitate and then build on success.
- Aimee decided to involve the students in charting and reflecting on their engagement, learning, and progress.
- Aimee decided that some writers needed individual, temporary scaffolds to help them settle into writing work.

Writing well requires time and it requires space in which writers can make and pursue plans. But writing well also requires support en route. The following cases demonstrate how writers can be supported in developing and encoding their ideas.

Writers Draw on Their Knowledge of Language(s): Using Multiple Languages When Writing

Meet Celia, Diego, and Evie. Celia is a third-grade writer in a transitional bilingual classroom, and Evie and Diego are first-grade writers in a bilingual classroom in the same school. Among other beliefs, their teachers' vision includes the promise and potential of their young writers to develop as bilingual and biliterate people. Therefore, children in their classes are initially encouraged to develop literacy skills in the language they know best and then, over time, to add English to their literacy knowledge. For Jessica, the first-grade teacher, this means beginning by engaging her students in writing in Spanish. For Andrea, Celia's third-grade teacher, it means inviting writers to draw on and use their Spanish and English depending on the writing piece, its purpose, and the author's intentions.

When studying how to write directions, first grader Evie wrote about her expertise in writer's workshop, informing readers that if they didn't know how to participate in writer's workshop, she could teach them (see Figure 3.13). Evie's literacy skills in Spanish are strong. She encodes her ideas with ease and uses sounds and the syllabic structure of Spanish to put her ideas to paper. When it comes to writing "Writer's Workshop," she has a go in English in her introduction—"RatosworhaP"—and then decides to use "W.W." in the title of the steps someone might take.

Figure 3.13: Learning to write well: Strengthening first language literacies.

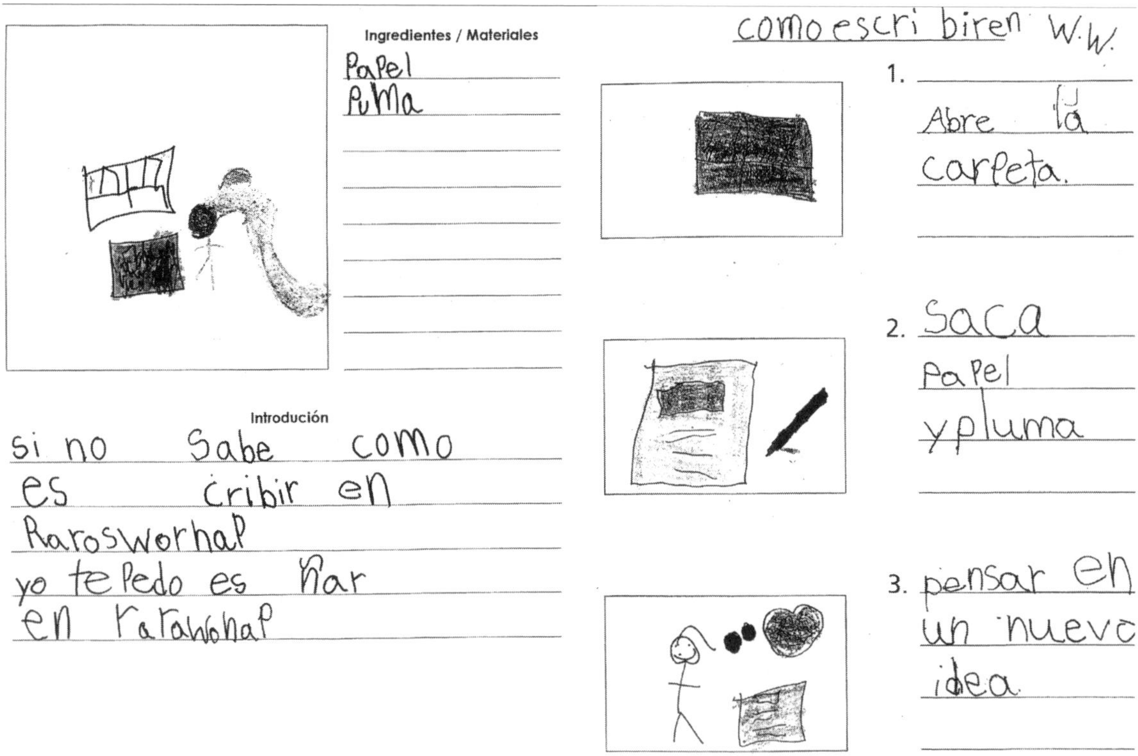

Ingredientes / Materiales

PaPel
PuMa

Introdución

Si no Sabe como
es cribir en
Rarosworhal
yo te Pedo es ñar
en rarawohaP

como escri biren W.W.

1. _____
Abre la
carPeta.

2. Saca
PaPel
y Pluma

3. pensar en
un nuevo
idea

Evie's classmate Diego is equally full of ideas. He loves writing time and talks with passion and energy about his ideas, which, during one day of this unit of study, involved how to brush one's teeth. Sitting at the table with other writers, Diego talked out his ideas in detail, subvocalizing as he wrote and then recording a short string of letters. The first step, *Pone el pasta en el cepillo de dientes* (put the toothpaste on the toothbrush), he first recorded as *Pnlap* (see Figure 3.14). Jessica, Diego's teacher, knew that Diego was hearing more sounds than he was writing, and also knew that Diego loved to produce lots of pieces during writer's workshop and so worked with great speed. She wondered how to help Diego put more information on his paper so that other people could read his texts. Sitting alongside Diego, Jessica began their conversation by noting how many words Diego was trying to write—eight in all. They looked at his paper, on which only one five-letter word appeared. Diego immediately recognized this as a problem. As Jessica and Diego worked together, he drew eight little lines on his paper. Next, Jessica asked Diego to identify the words that seemed bigger to him; he immediately identified *pone*, *pasta*, *cepillo*, and *dientes* as bigger words, so they drew bigger boxes for the bigger words and smaller boxes for the smaller words. Jessica then asked him to fill in the boxes with all the sounds he heard for each of the words he was writing. She then let Diego move on to the next steps independently. When left alone, he returned to writing "his way." Jessica, however, made this strategy a focus of her teaching with Diego over the following days and weeks.

Down the hall, Celia was using her developing biliteracy skills in a different way. As she sat down to write in her notebook early in her third-grade year, Celia decided to write about getting ready for a recent trip with her dad. She wrote the entry with ease and decided to use a short snippet of dialogue in her piece. In a conference, Celia shared the thinking behind the words on the page. She'd decided to infuse Spanish into her English-dominant entry, noting that "it's because my dad speaks just Spanish." As the conference continued, Celia used her talk to think aloud and eventually concluded that it was important for any character, or real person, to talk in stories just like they talk and sound in real life. In this case, Celia was able to arrive at a general tenet to guide future writing decisions from a single decision she'd made inside daily notebook writing (see Figure 3.15).

Figure 3.14: Supporting first language literacy development: Creating scaffolds.

While all three writers used diverse languages, how they used them and what they and their teachers decided about using them varied. Among the decisions made:

- Both teachers decided that developing students' literacy skills in both languages mattered, and that kids should be involved in deciding which language to use when and where, as well as deciding what their language should look like on the page so that readers could access their thinking.

- Diego's teacher decided to push Diego to put more of what he knew on paper by using word boxes as scaffolds.

- Evie decided to try some writing in English, and after two solid attempts, opted to use abbreviations to ensure readers understood what she meant.

Figure 3.15: Using just the right words: Communicating character traits using multiple languages.

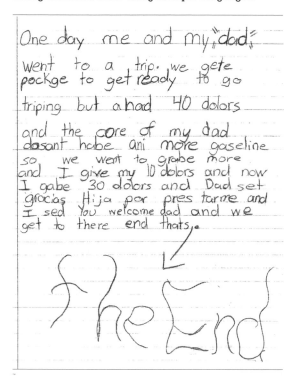

- Celia decided to use her knowledge of Spanish to accurately portray a person's speech in her writing.

Successful writers are supported by their teachers, especially as students learn to compose in multiple languages. Another way teachers support their young writers is through the use of models. The next case demonstrates how one teacher encouraged her students to turn to the writing of their peers in order to help their own writing.

Writers Use Models: Using Other Writing to Assist in Composing

Fourth grader Lindsay looks to models to help her compose, but in her case the models come from the work of her peers. In one unit of study, as Lindsay and her classmates wrote focused personal narratives, their teacher noticed the differences in how her young writers were beginning their pieces. Selena began:

> My mom was picking me up from school and she was just at the hospital with my brother Jordan and my dad. My mother's cell phone rang it was the hospital and my dad turned the car around, my mom started to cry. I was scared. My heart was racing. Was someone sick? Was someone hurt? I was speechless. I wasn't sure what was going on. Then I looked at Jordan and he was asleep, but his skin was yellow. . . .

Another classmate began:

> I've had many friends come to Michigan, but I'll always remember when Christopher came.

Other writers were more direct, like Lindsay. Her piece initially began, "One day at my grandparents house . . . I learned how to dive." Her piece continued with a step-by-step recounting of learning to dive. While her teacher could have used literature to illustrate how authors might draw readers into a piece, she used peer writing instead. Lindsay's teacher, Katie, turned to peer writing as model texts because she thought that peer writing provided students with attainable models, the kind that would encourage them to think, "If my friend can do it, so can I."

During a conference, Lindsay told Katie that she was trying to use Selena's opening to help her, and she referenced the notes she'd taken during that day's mini-lesson (see Figure 3.16). They talked about how Selena's opening made the reader wonder what was going on, and Lindsay came to understand that this was what she wanted to do in her own work. After the conference, Lindsay had a few more minutes to write and began a new opening for her piece. When independent writing time came to a close, Lindsay shared her initial revisions with her classmates:

Lindsay: I did a lead sentence about when I first learned how to dive.

Katie: What did you use to help you?

Lindsay: I used Selena's words.

Katie: She took Selena's opening where she gave the reader lots of information to get the reader wondering before coming out and saying what her topic is going to be. Lindsay is trying to set the scene like Selena did. Do you want to share what you have so far?

Lindsay: I am the youngest cousin out of my whole family and I am the last one to know how to dive. This summer, something happened. . . .

When reading aloud her revision, Lindsay made another change. On paper, her second sentence was still emerging and she had written, "Every summer . . ." and then she stopped for the day. Lindsay was beginning to understand what it meant to use models to help herself grow as a writer. Her teacher helped her not only revise her beginning but also articulate what she was doing. Through conferences and the opportunity to share, Lindsay inched closer to developing an opening that kept the reader wondering. While she might not be "there" yet, Lindsay was coming to see herself as someone who could turn to her peers, borrow a strategy or technique, try it out herself, and better engage readers with her written work.

To successfully use peer writing as model texts, Lindsay and her teacher made a number of decisions:

- Lindsay's teacher decided that using student examples honored the successes of writers in the classroom, positioned particular writers as people to turn to for help with a particular skill, and provided examples that were within reach of other writers in the classroom.

- Lindsay decided that her lead needed work.

- Lindsay's teacher decided to invite Lindsay to share her decisions as a means of helping Lindsay make explicit the decisions she'd made, as well as showing others a real example of how the day's focus had helped writers in their classroom.

Figure 3.16: Beginning pieces: Using student beginnings to teach classmates.

What do writers do to set the scene when they're drafting?

Writer	Beginning lines	Notes about what this writer did to set the scene…
Heather	*I've had many friends at my Michigan house, but I'll always remember when Christopher came.*	*Writer starts with all of the times something has happened,* but then tells the reader they're going to write about ONE time.
Sabina	Were you ever an aunt at the age of nine? Most people say that's weird. But for me, having a niece at the age of nine is normal.	She asked a question she told her own connection.
Emmett	My hands are stinging from squeezing the chair that now felt like sharp metal. I was nervous. I could very slightly hear my class cheering for me. I couldn't hear much I was too nervous. It seemed like I was covering my ears. I was in the school-wide spelling bee.	He told the Reader how he feels and he keeps the reader wondering.
Selena	My mom was picking me up from school and she was just at the hospital with my brother Jayden and my dad. My mother's cell phone rang it was the hospital, my dad turned the car around, my mom started to cry. I was scared. My heart was racing. Was someone sick? Was someone hurt? I was speechless. I wasn't sure what was going on. Then I looked at Jayden and he was asleep, but his skin was yellow…	Keeps the reader wondering. Very Deciptive.

What do writers do to set the scene when they're drafting?

Writer	Beginning lines	Notes about what this writer did to set the scene…
Heather	*I've had many friends at my Michigan house, but I'll always remember when Christopher came.*	*Writer starts with all of the times something has happened,* but then tells the reader they're going to write about ONE time.
Sabina	Were you ever an aunt at the age of nine? Most people say that's weird. But for me, having a niece at the age of nine is normal.	• She made a question and Then she • gave what she though or own Cruction
Emmett	My hands are stinging from squeezing the chair that now felt like sharp metal. I was nervous. I could very slightly hear my class cheering for me. I couldn't hear much I was too nervous. It seemed like I was covering my ears. I was in the school-wide spelling bee.	• he leaves the reader wondering • he ses his, ae sing
Selena	My mom was picking me up from school and she was just at the hospital with my brother Jayden and my dad. My mother's cell phone rang it was the hospital, my dad turned the car around, my mom started to cry. I was scared. My heart was racing. Was someone sick? Was someone hurt? I was speechless. I wasn't sure what was going on. Then I looked at Jayden and he was asleep, but his skin was yellow…	• she keep the reader wondering • she give questing • She uses ••• • Very discriped

While Lindsay was using a classmate's text as a mentor, she was also revising her draft in ways that moved beyond adding a word or deleting a sentence. For far too many young people, drafting means writing a piece from beginning to end, and revising means merely changing words (perhaps using a thesaurus in the process) and recopying text again and again in multiple drafts—more of a handwriting and copying exercise than a thinking activity. The next case focuses on other ways we might help young people revise texts as they engage in ongoing composing processes.

Writers Revise: Learning and Practicing Revision Tools

Meet Demetrio, a member of a third-and-fourth-grade transitional bilingual classroom. On a day when his teacher invited students to use their notebooks to develop focused entries, Demetrio chose to write about his brother. He began:

> My brother was a good student. He's out of school, all the way out of school. He wanted to go into the Army but my Dad didn't want him to. . . .

When the teacher approached Demetrio for a conference, Demetrio's page was a little more than half full, and he was beginning to draw a person (see Figure 3.17):

Teacher: Talk to me about the work you're doing right now.

Demetrio: It's about my brother.

Teacher: I noticed you were doing something down here [pointing to the drawing near the bottom of the entry]; tell me what you are doing down here.

Demetrio: I was going to do my brother.

Teacher: Why are you going to draw your brother? How is it helping your writing work to draw your brother?

Demetrio: Because I like him and write about him.

Teacher: You can use that sketch to help yourself write more and include more information for your reader. As you add details to your drawing, you can go back and reread your writing to see if you included details that you remember as you sketch. And if you find you didn't include some of the information you remember now, you can use a caret. Do you know about carets?

Demetrio: No? ¿zanahoria?

Teacher: A different kind [zanahoria = carrot]. I'm not exactly sure how to say it in Spanish; we'll have to find out. It's a little mark that we use to add in the information so you don't have to

Figure 3.17: Using revision tools.

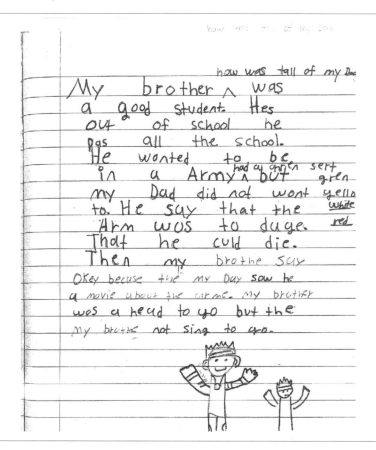

erase when you want to add more in the middle of what you've
already written. From your drawing, tell me something about
your brother.

Demetrio: He's big, he already finished school.

Teacher: So he already graduated. Let's reread to see if you have that
information in your writing.

Demetrio: My brother was a good student. He's out of school, all the way
out of school.

Teacher: So you have the part about your brother finishing school. How
about the part about how big your brother is?

Demetrio: He's almost as tall as my dad.

> **Teacher:**   Where can you put that in your writing? *[pointing, the teacher demonstrates how to use a caret]*

Demetrio began to add information about his brother's size and then returned to sketching, adding patches to the arm of his brother's shirt. During independent writing, Demetrio added information about his brother's green shirt and the different colors on the arm. During sharing time, when Demetrio's work was highlighted, his teacher and peers noticed that his notebook contained another caret with additional information about shirt color and the color of the bands on the arm, but that he had not yet mentioned what the bands are called. A peer suggested the word *patches* to describe the bands of color stitched on to his brother's Army shirt.

In the conference with his teacher, Demetrio was offered a tool to move him from the role of illustrator to the role of writer who uses sketches and carets to revise the ideas written on the page. When his work was made public, he gained assistance from peers as well, finding just the right word in English to describe the detail he'd included in his picture. And an ensuing investigation revealed that *flecha* or *signo de inserción* could be used to refer to the caret that writers use.

In this case, revision tools and strategies were tremendously helpful in encouraging Demetrio to extend and develop his writing. To get there, he and his teacher made some important decisions:

- Demetrio's teacher decided to view sketching as a tool that could be used in writing and revision processes.
- Demetrio's teacher decided to teach him a way to add more writing that didn't involve erasing or recopying text.
- Demetrio decided to use details that emerged from his drawing and writing in his text.
- Demetrio and his teacher decided to investigate how writers might refer to carets in Spanish.

Learning some revision strategies and tools is one way to help writers; another way, as illustrated in the next classroom, is discovering how punctuation is more than a list of rules—it's a way to clarify meaning.

Writers Guide Readers: Using Punctuation to Control Readings

Randy is a fourth-grade writer who regularly thinks and writes with his second-grade poetry pal. Randy's teacher is fond of using poetry as a tool for teaching and learning about language. The class begins each day with a new poem and student-led discussion about the poem—its content, structure, the poet's possible lines of thinking when he or she wrote the poem, and so on. Kids keep poetry notebooks with diverse collections of poems; the teacher intentionally encourages students to reach beyond rhyming poems and formulaic poems such as acrostics and haiku. Fourth graders also convene weekly with second-grade poetry pals to read, discuss, and write poetry.

Early in the school year, after Randy and his poetry pal had spent time reading poetry, Randy asked his partner if he was interested in writing a poem.

> We both started thinking about stuff we both like. We picked Mario Karts. He [Randy's second-grade partner] helped to [give] me ideas to write about because we both like the game. We put in characters from the game—[the game] basically has characters like Wario, Bauser, DK, Peach, and some more racing carts. They dodge obstacles like piranha plants and cheep cheeps. We added seaweed because we needed more ideas.

After explaining the process of generating ideas and content for the poem, Randy went on to explain their intentions for the poem and how punctuation and form helped them reach their goals (see Figure 3.18).

> We wrote so people would think they're actually in it—we wrote it like a race. I was acting like I was the host of it. It's a poem, not like this [shows narrative notebook entry]; it's not justified. Well, it has different lines—some are long; some aren't. I added a comma here [right after we find out Peach is in last place] to slow down the race. The lower half goes slower 'til it gets to the exciting part ["Mario Luigi Mario Luigi Mario Luigi"], then it goes fast again.

When asked what made the reader go fast again, Randy talked about the absence of commas, periods, or three dots (not yet knowing the terminology for an ellipsis but being well aware of its function). He explained that adding commas between the names would make the pace too slow: "It's an exciting end to the race; you don't know who'll win to the last moment." He then read the line rapidly, expressing the tension of not knowing who would win until the last possible second.

Learning to use punctuation as a way to further meaning became an important revision strategy for Randy and his partner. To get there, he and his teacher made some decisions:

- Randy's teacher decided to use genuine writerly language—such as *justification*—when talking about writing forms and practices, knowing that writers need to understand and use these words when talking with other writers.
- Randy's teacher decided that engaging students in rich reading and extensive experience with language and how it's used aids in developing what young writers do.
- Randy and his writing partner decided that collaboration and using what they knew well (the Mario Karts game) would help them write well.
- Randy and his poetry pal decided to use punctuation and form to control how readers would interact with their poem.

Figure 3.18: Controlling readers: Randy and his poetry pal make just the right punctuation decisions.

Mario Karts

All the Mario kart drivers wait.
6 of 8 drivers start out late.
Mario & Luigi are in the lead
All the sudden they're stuck in seaweed.
Bowser gets up way ahead
Then he got hit by a shell in the head.
Poor peach is in last place,
And then she got a bullet bill to pick up the pace.
As for toad that's in 7th place, then he got a star
& got real far.
The Mario kart drivers are on lap 2,
Just then Mario lost his shoe.
Wario came up real fast,
Then Bowser hit him with a shell now he's last.
DK's in 2nd, Luigi's in 1st, Now Mario's in 2nd DK
Says HEY!!
In 1st Mario Luigi Mario Luigi Mario Luigi Mario Luigi.........IT'S A
TIE
!!!!!!!!!!!!!!!!!! At the finish line they say hi.

On paper, we see some of what Randy knows as writer. His talk opens additional windows onto his knowledge and ability to make intentional decisions in his writing to shape how readers interact with his text. His talk reveals his understanding of the functions of punctuation. Periods are more than marks that "must go" at the end of sentences. Rather, they're signs that let readers know when to stop and pause, stops that are longer than those suggested by commas. Randy also knows that ". . ." plays a role in pacing readers. Though he might not have had explicit instruction on this punctuation, he's been part of a classroom that always tunes in to the *why* behind writing decisions and he's read enough to enable him to figure out the function before the term. While there is no ellipsis in his writing and no commas in the final Mario Luigi line, Randy's poetry-writing experience signals the importance of reflective talk in understanding a writer's thinking, as well as providing insight into what he chose *not* to use in his writing work.

In many ways, this concluding case is a good lead into Chapter 4. Simply looking at student work on paper or on screen often falls short of telling us what kids know, are thinking, and are deciding as they engage in writing work. We often need other ways to engage with them so that we can see the thinking that has informed their actions, just as listening to Randy talk about his punctuation decisions illuminated the poem on the page. We also need ways to teach kids not only how to engage in productive writing work but also how to be cognizant of what they're doing, when, and why. In other words, we need to teach them how to reflect on their own processes, practices, and decisions.

Becoming Aware: Learning to See and Own Writing Decisions

Teacher: Have you ever used a quote before to inspire your writing?

Evelyn: No, never. Until now.

Teacher: How did that work for you?

Evelyn: I thought that it was very, very, very good. I actually didn't get very much in one day but I could keep writing about it. [I could] probably [get more quotes] from songs. . . .

Fourth grader Evelyn's recent efforts to use a quote to launch her writing reveals not only that she is willing to try new things as she engages in this work, but also that she has an awareness of how things are going and, given her experiences, what she might do next (see Figure 4.1). I spoke with Evelyn just after her teacher had invited students to choose one of three quotes as inspiration for composing an entry in their writer's notebook. As a means of teaching kids how writers might get ideas or get going, this strategy appealed to Evelyn, who not only found it to be useful on that given day but also was already thinking about where she could get more quotes to inspire more writing.

Figure 4.1: Using quotes to launch writing and thinking.

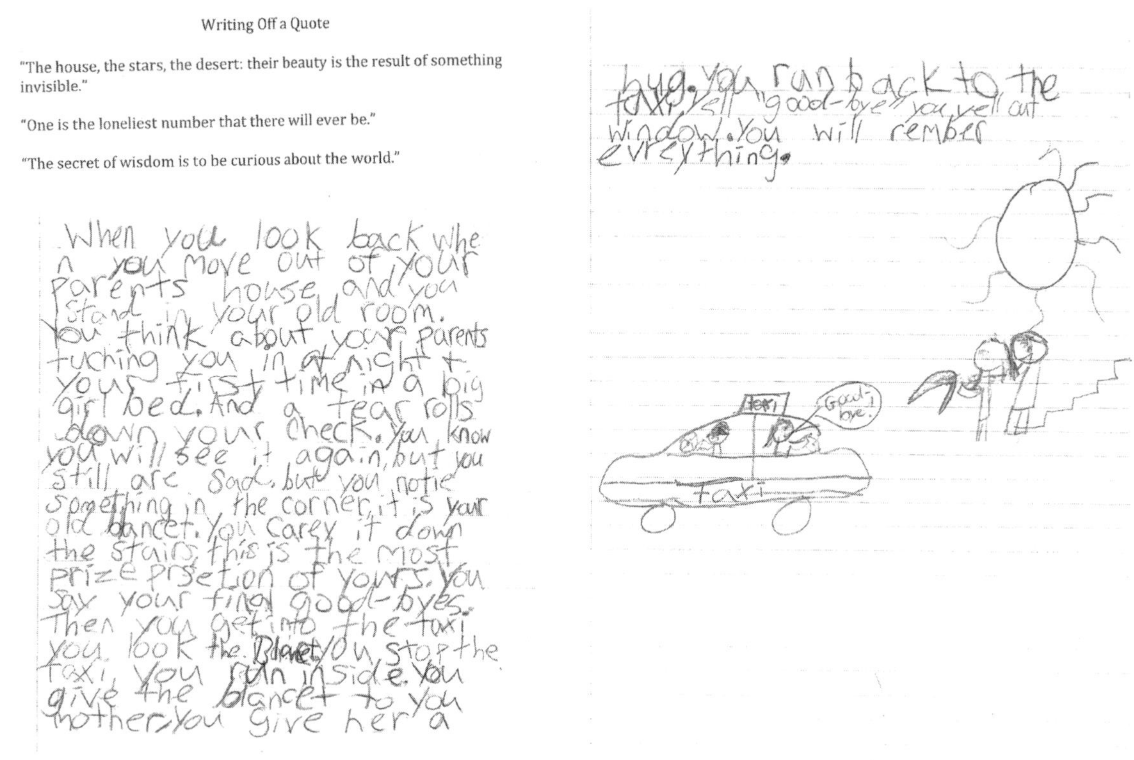

Writing Off a Quote

"The house, the stars, the desert: their beauty is the result of something invisible."

"One is the loneliest number that there will ever be."

"The secret of wisdom is to be curious about the world."

When you look back when you move out of your parents house and you stand in your old room. You think about your parents tuching you in at night + your first time in a big girl bed. And a tear rolls down your check. You know you will see it again, but you still are sad. but you notie something in the corner, it is your old blancet. You carey it down the stairs, this is the most prize prsetion of yours. You say your final good-byes. Then you get into the taxi you look the. Plaet you stop the taxi, you run inside. You give the blancet to you mother. You give her a

hug. You run back to the taxi, yell "good-bye" you yell out window. You will rember everything.

Writers like Evelyn and those featured in Chapter 3 have spent time in classrooms where writing instruction has intentionally focused on making and articulating wise decisions. These young writers have learned, in the company of their teachers and classmates, how to become strategic writers who learn not only how to write well but also how to see their thinking en route. Writers don't come to us as strategic, self-aware composers experienced in explaining their thinking; rather, writers learn how to see and put into words what they have learned through instruction and experience. This chapter attends to how writers and their teachers have worked together to unpack the processes of writing in ways that allow them to produce good writing as well as to understand *how* they are able to do so. These students have developed metacognitive practices that help them both to complete tasks and to see the possibilities (or challenges) of using particular practices in future writing. And given their awareness of what they do and why they do it, they are better equipped to make intentional and effective decisions as they continue to use writing to think, reflect, communiciate, and make their voices heard.

How can we help young people see and learn from and along their journeys? How can we teach them to attend not only to the products they make but also to the processes they engage with? How do we help them recognize writing as a series of decisions and learn to articulate the decisions they have made? The truth is that there are many ways to do this. What follows, however, are illustrations of the practices that teachers I've collaborated with have used to help their students see what they're doing and take ownership of the decisions they make—and, along the way, come to know themselves better as writers and be better prepared to write well.

Creating the Right Conditions

Before we begin to help young writers see and take ownership of the decisions they make, we need to take several initial steps to make sure writers are working in conditions that expect as well as support thinking about their thought processes—often referred to as metacognitive reflection. Writers need to be surrounded with supportive peers and mentors; they need deep understandings of quality writing, including the complexities of writing work; they need opportunties, as well as guidance, to take responsibility for what and how they write; and they need to know when to stick with a line of thinking or a project and when it makes more sense to change their minds and perhaps start anew. Conditions such as these encourage writers not only to *do* work but also to take ownership of their learning. Part of our job is to offer instruction that introduces writers to new options and strategies, and to introduce strategies that help learners reflect on and monitor their own experiences so that they become better directors of their own learning, thinking, and writing processes. The following sections offer examples and explanations of how teachers have endeavored to construct supportive communities in which writers value challenging themselves and stepping outside their comfort zones to take on new, more sophisticated practices; in which they understand quality writing and writerly work; in which young writers take responsibility for writing well by making intentional choices about and within the projects they pursue; and in which they understand the balance between working through hard parts and starting over, launching something new, or taking a break.

> **Helping Young Writers in Their Journey: Creating the Right Conditions**
>
> - Constructing supportive writing communities
> - Helping students understand quality writing
> - Teaching students to take responsibility: Making and owning choices
> - Persevering and calling it quits: Knowing when to stick with it and when to walk away

Constructing Supportive Writing Communities

It's risky to share one's thinking or make visible the decisions one is making either through writing or talk. Writers may feel vulnerable and may worry about wanting to seem "right" versus making visible the productive and sometimes not-so-productive decisions they've made. Being honest matters. If we are to move beyond what we currently know and can do, we need to challenge ourselves and be okay with admitting when something isn't working or when something is hard and we need help or more experience to improve. Although we learn from our successes, we also learn when things don't work for us. And it might even be that we learn more from our mistakes than from our successes. Consider, for example, what taking risks meant in Mitch's life. Sixth grader Mitch was an accomplished writer and someone who saw himself as a leader in his fourth-through-sixth-grade multiage classroom. Mitch wrote fine poetry with ease, turned out initial drafts that were more developed than those of most of his peers, and saw himself as someone who was academically successful. However, taking risks and positioning himself as someone who could learn from others was often a challenge for him. For example, on one occasion when Mitch made a presentation to the class, he used some very basic technological tools. When asked if there were ways to enhance his presentation, he initially avoided the notion of revision, as well as the idea that he didn't know enough about technology to present his material differently. As the class responded to his work, they wondered if Nina (a younger classmate with less English language experience but greater technological skills) could help Mitch in further developing his presentation and thinking. Eventually he signed on, took a needed risk, and asked for Nina's assistance. As they worked alongside each other, Nina watched what Mitch could do already and then offered demonstrations of new options. Together they created a richer presentation, deepened each other's understandings of the topic, and learned that taking risks, while difficult, often moves learners to new places.

I know this to be true in my own writing life when I get feedback on a manuscript. Rarely is a manuscript accepted as is, and editors' questions, insights, and feedback push me to rethink concepts, organization, language, etc. In the end, both the piece and my own thinking practices have improved. Mitch's willingness to work with Nina and my practice of sending off a piece of writing for others to read and critique are the kinds of risks we need to take if we are to move beyond where we currently stand as learners, writers, and people. Such risks are much easier to take if embedded in supportive writing communities where we, along with others, are invested in continued growth.

And so, if part of our vision is that learners, and specifically writers, need to take risks in order to critically reflect, we need to create supportive environments in which such growth and reflection can happen. We need to make the time to create a healthy classroom community. In supportive communities, members know one another. They share stories, celebrate accomplishments together, and check in to make sure things are okay or at least getting better. In supportive classroom communities, the interests and passions of both kids and teachers are topics of learning. We, just as much as kids, need to be reflected in our classrooms. When students see us living as passionate, engaged learners and writers, engagement is often contagious.

So how do we create supportive writing communities? Recently, while talking with a first-grade teacher about her efforts to ensure that writing instruction was embedded in a healthy learning environment, I learned about her decision to reintroduce morning journals, a practice she had abandoned in an effort to focus on creating a writing workshop in her classroom. She explained that although the schedule allowed for dedicated times in the week for focused study and engagement with writing as students studied poetry, nonfiction, and other genres, she noticed that kids wanted to know more about one another and wanted to tell more about their own lives. She realized that to meet that need, she would have to create a regular time and space in which students could share what was on their minds. Now, soon after the kids enter the classroom, they settle into breakfast, writing, and sharing, because they "have so much to say."

Making the time to let kids share important moments in their lives went a long way toward creating a community of support in this teacher's classroom. And while chances are we're not going to squeeze more time out of our weeks, we need to find ways for kids to develop a sense of belonging, for them to know that their thinking and lives are valued. This teacher found morning journals to be a good option for building a caring, inclusive learning community. But there are other options as well. We might, for example, invite students and their families to participate in at-home written conversation notebooks in which kids and family members write back and forth regularly about topics of their own choosing in the languages they're most comfortable using. Written conversation notebooks could serve as a window into the lives of kids and families beyond school walls, providing insights that we can then wrap into classroom learning. When teachers are active participants in the classroom community, we can further build relationships with young people and their families. We might create a designated space for each child on a classroom bulletin board as kindergarten teacher Sabrina did, with each student in charge of what is on display in his or her square. As they post particular pieces of work, newspaper clippings, photos, drawings, etc., their cares and interests become more visible and our interactions and teaching decisions are better informed.

Whether we use morning journals, written conversation notebooks, student display centers, or other techniques to construct our classroom communities, we can build on this foundatation of care and trust as we invite kids to talk and write, not just about events, ideas, or issues in their lives but also about their thinking processes and practices.

Helping Students Understand Quality Writing

Once student writers are living in a supportive writing community, it is essential for them to develop shared understandings of what it means to be a successful writer who writes well. Before students can write well or be strategic in their decision making, they need to know why they are writing, what they can compose, and what strategies they might use, even as they begin to name their own preferences for particular processes.

All too often, visions of writing well are tied to a step-by-step process and to specific products and artifacts. Rather than talking about how and when they revise scenes, or drawing on real-life examples or research to bring a character or piece to life, students who live and write in writing-as-a-singular-linear-process type of environment mistakenly equate writing well with completing specific steps. When asked, for example, what they do when they write, they might respond that first they "prewrite" or "brainstorm." When asked to explain what they mean by these popular terms, students often fall silent or perhaps respond that they should make a web illustrating core ideas. This web might then be taken as evidence that the writer has thought through his or her ideas before writing and thus has an understanding of his or her own processes as a writer. Similarly, some teachers view an error-free piece (i.e., the writing displays conventional spelling and correct punctuation and paragraphing) with no voice or passion as quality writing. Chapter 5 will dig more deeply into how we establish some shared definitions of what it means to become a strategic and strong writer, but we know that writing well involves much more than making webs or correcting spelling. We need to make sure that young writers understand this too, that we encourage them to move beyond creating safe pieces—those that are intentionally short, those that include only words they can spell with confidence, and those that stick to simple declarative sentences that students know how to punctuate properly.

Consider how differently Evelyn defines quality writing. In talking with me about her notebook entry featured in the opening of this chapter, Evelyn noted that she began with the following quote selected from three offered to the class by their teacher: "The house, the stars, the desert: their beauty is the result of something invisible." This quote made her think about the possibility of an impending move for her family and what it might be like to leave her house, bedroom, and blanket behind. She went on to explain:

"The house, the stars, the desert, their beauty the result of something invisible." Well, the part about my blanket, well, I actually have a blanket that I love very, very much. Well, that blanket, "their beauty the result of something invisible" comes in there. Not many people, well to some people, it would just be a blanket, but to me—

I decided since I was maybe going to move I wanted to get that feeling, so people [reading] know what might happen and how you might feel. . . . [I wrote] "when you"—I wan[ted to] write this as something people can read and they can refer to them so that they can picture themselves and not imagine a character in their minds, but put them in it.

I [also] put a lot of depth into my writing. . . . Like, there's a quote, *[skimming through her piece to find the example quote from her own writing that she is thinking about]* there's a something I wrote down here *[on finding the quote, she reads from her entry]*, "and a tear rolled down your cheek." It's like depth, detail.

For Evelyn, writing well was about having a vision and knowing what steps she could take to get herself there. Quality was about depth, detail, involving readers through the use of second person, and calling on readers to reflect on what they might feel in this situation. If we share and expand on Evelyn's vision of quality writing as writing that makes readers reflect, cry, laugh, change their minds, or ask new questions, we will define quality writing in increasingly complex ways, recognizing how important it is for writers to strategically make more sophisticated decisions (such as using second person, using examples to show emotion, incorporating internal monologue, writing from a perspective other than their own, inserting quotes in their work). And for the vision I—and many of my colleagues—hold about writing, this more complex stance captures well what quality writing is all about.

To help students develop a sense of what it means to engage in quality writing work, when they come to me with their writing in hand and ask the inevitable question, "Is this good?," my first response, without even looking at their work, is, "Tell me what you mean by 'good.'" I then listen, and use their definition to turn the tables. If they tell me that good writing "tells about something the writer is interested in," "has pictures that go with the words," or "tells the reader all the details," I ask them to reread their work to see if their topic is something they're interested in, if their pictures go with their words, or if they have provided their reader with adequate details. Depending on their response and my thinking about their development as a writer, if they answer yes to the questions posed, I may then ask them to show me where and how they've included needed details or to explain why their pictures go with their words. While there certainly are times when I share my thinking and opinions, I want kids to develop an internal sense of what is good and what is or isn't working for them.

Becoming a writer who writes well and who actually uses writing for a variety of purposes calls for an understanding of writing as a process—a process with lots of hard parts, uncertainties, and opportunities to hone and clarify one's thinking and have an impact on a variety of readers. Figuring out one's own processes, including strategies used to start, choose, develop, change, and polish writing, requires experience in looking back, seeing what one has done, assessing the quality of one's efforts thus far, naming the hard parts, and deciding what to do to move foward. It's not easy and it grows from and with experience—experience embedded in safe spaces filled with supportive teaching practices.

Teaching Students to Take Responsibility: Making and Owning Choices

Another important consideration when creating communities of reflective writers who understand, articulate, and own the decisions they make is the issue of responsibility and ownership. Young people need to have opportunities to make choices—in terms of the topics they write about, the ways they write about them, and the paths they pursue to craft particular pieces. While at times teaching may attend to particular genres or be connected with other content areas like social studies that then define a range of topics writers will be writing about, we can't make all the decisions for kids. If we do, the only thing they learn about writing is to follow directions.

Furthermore, if we want young people to spend extended stretches of time engaged in writing, they have to be invested in that work. I recently found a journal I had written in fifth grade. Each page was filled with responses to the teacher's prompts—why I liked Halloween, what I wanted to be when I grew up, and why I thought the "Beaver Rules" (the beaver was the school mascot) were good. Each prompt evoked a compliant, one-paragraph response. I'm not so sure I liked the Beaver Rules, but that's not what I wrote. And I'm quite certain that if I'd been asked to write an essay on the merits of the Beaver Rules, I would have resented every moment I was required to work on it and my goal would have been to "be done," as it was with the journal entry, rather than to engage with it as a serious writer with a mission. Fortunately, there are other classrooms in which students make decisions about the content of their pieces, and it shows in the quality of their writing and thinking.

One day as third- and fourth-grade students were beginning to explore nonfiction writing, their teacher asked them to consider what they knew best and therefore might pursue in their writing. As a Chihuahua owner and the person in her family charged with her dog's care, Ainslie immediately began a notebook entry that detailed how to care for a Chihuahua. Not only did the entry capture information about bathing and exercise, but Ainslee's voice, care, and commitment to writing well were also evident (see Figure 4.2). A few months later, when the class began to explore essays, classmates chose topics close to their hearts. While some wrote about family issues, others began drafting about the presence and danger of gangs in the community. The genres and topics shifted, but student commitment remained strong. And down the hall, as sixth graders were called to write an in-class essay, Trevor's decision to write about moving back in with his father and meeting his father's girlfriend did much more than allow him to relay events and comply with assignment requirements. Using carefully crafted words, he captured a difficult time in his life (see Figure 4.3), and his honesty, voice, and skills as a writer are evident.

Figure 4.2: Connecting choice and quality writing in a third- and fourth-grade classroom.

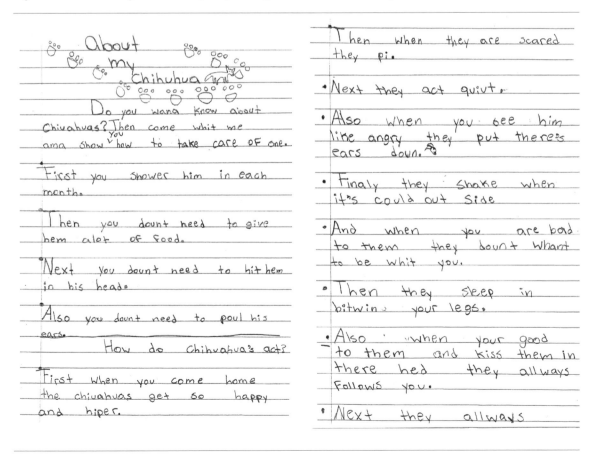

Figure 4.3: Connecting choice and quality in a sixth-grade classroom.

Early August, I'm finally here father, four years of separation with my mother and I end up staying with you again. When I think about it I didn't do much that day, woke up, brushed my teeth, the phone rang with your caller I.D. As I stepped out the car, my father stood there with a smile, but something was wrong, who is that lady with the spectacles & fuzzy hair, I wanted to scream, why is she here father, why is she here. Such a defile ounce from me lady.

After my grandmother left, my father told me the lady's name is Vicky, maybe it was me or that name was deadly. I still felt strange, why was she here, they showed me my bedroom. A boy much taller than me, walked up to me with no expression and he whispered to the lady, the sight of him sickens me, who were they, my question was answered. My stepmother & stepbrother, that was right when my dad left for work. The lady shut the door nice and quiet, turned and faced me with a devilish look or maybe her face was back. She went into the kitchen, grabbed a scrub, and threw to me, she told me to wash the carpet I had dirtied when I entered. A simple request, tiresome for a 5 year-old boy however, I scrubbed & scrubbed, her reaction was anger she beat me for no reason, I was in pain and shocked.

Retribution was not served before I went to bed, she asked for me to massage her and if I fell asleep and she woke up and saw me, there was no mercy. What did this lady want, has she gone mad?! Her field was more friendly so my stay was of more ease.

In Conclusion, the torture never ceased, every passing day made my body ache. My only comfort was my father always playing video games with me, taking me out to eat. Unfortunately, how good things are drowned by bad, but this was definitely one strange day, which lasted eight months …

Ainslie and Trevor and their classmates were willing to commit to writing that pulled readers in to their texts, their lives, and their thinking in genuine ways. If we want kids to think reflectively about why they started a piece in a particular way, why they chose to include a quote from their grandmother, why they wrote a poem instead of an essay or an article, how they came to modify spellings as they moved closer to publication, or why they chose to write about pressing community and social issues, students need to be invested in what they write. And for us, the pedagogical imperative is to find ways to teach students how to make good choices.

Persevering and Calling It Quits: Knowing When to Stick with It and When to Walk Away

Once we help young writers know how to make good choices as they write, we need to help them recognize the role of honest thinking as they move forward. This means helping kids move beyond the need to be "right" and craft "perfect" or "always great" stories, poems, and articles. Some of the things we write don't initially turn out to be strong. Perhaps we need to spend more time drafting and revising in order to improve them. Perhaps some projects need to be put away for a while and then revisited after some time has passed. Perhaps regardless of the amount of time we put in, some pieces will never have the impact we intend. Whatever the case, kids need to know that perseverance is a real part of writing work, that good writers try to identify the places in their writing that aren't working, either on their own or with the help of others, and then try to make them better. Not getting it right from the start is not the sign of a bad writer—it's normal. And just as kids need to work in environments that support and value perseverance, they need to know that it's okay to walk away from a piece that simply isn't working out. Just as not getting it right from the start is normal, so too is shifting gears and beginning anew—as long writers don't constantly walk away from projects when difficultes arise.

When our students are invested in what they're writing about, when they care about the people they're writing with, when they know that there are regular, sustained times in their days when they can write, when they know that sticking with projects through the hard parts is valuable and that sometimes it's okay to walk away and start something new—then we can begin to teach, support, and expect that writers will learn to see and own their processes.

Learning to See Behind-the-Text Thinking

Both thinking about writing and writing well mean knowing what works for you and what doesn't. It means knowing about things you might do to get started, what

Learning to See Behind-the-Text Thinking

- Exploring the thinking behind published authors' texts

- Seeing the thinking behind peers' texts

you might do when you get stuck, how you might support your ideas within your writing, and so on. That might mean using quotes as Evelyn did to generate possible writing topics, responding to newspaper articles as Milo did to move beyond personal stories (see Chapter 3), or using punctuation as Randy did to control how readers engage with poetry (see Chapter 3). It also means not just solving writing problems but posing problems as well— that is, identifying where and what the hard parts are before you try to deal with them. And, finally, it means knowing how to think like a writer in multiple contexts so that you can always learn more about the many possible responses to writing difficulties. This section explores how we can help young writers learn to see the thinking behind others' texts, as well as help them to see how classmates might respond to identified writing challenges.

Exploring the Thinking behind Published Authors' Texts

We can begin to help kids see and articulate *their* thinking by helping them unpack *other writers'* thinking. For many teachers with whom I work, this means helping students understand the various ways they can approach a text: as reader-who-enjoys, as reader-who-responds, and even as reader-who-hypothesizes about the text's genesis and construction process. Students need to learn to read texts in multiple ways, focusing their attention initially on what is happening in the story; their reactions, connections, and disconnections from the story; and then questions that arise from their readings. They also need to read texts as writers (Fletcher, 1992; Ray, 1999), shifting their attention from what a story is about to why a writer might have written a particular piece and how the writer structured and shared his or her thinking. When students are invited to engage in reading as writers, they ask themselves questions such as these: Why did the writer write this? What sort of experiences would a writer have to have in order to write this? What do I see about how the writer crafted the words on the page? Reading as writers is, according to one team of teachers, about "sounding like a broken record and constantly thinking aloud as you, as reader and teacher, consume and produce texts alongside students." Taking multiple stances as text consumers can help young writers view the decisions made by other writers as potential choices they can make in their own texts.

Let me illustrate how you might go about this as a teacher. During a read-aloud, you might ask these kinds of questions: What do you suppose school was like for Sara Pennypacker, author of the book *Clementine* (2006)? I wonder if she got in trouble like her character Clementine does. If so, how do you suppose she used her own experiences to write this book? Let's find out. Or, what do you suppose Walter Dean Myers (2009) is hoping readers think about while reading *Looking Like Me*? Or, looking closer at his ways with words, you might hypothesize with students about why he used a repetitive structure. Or, during a morning meeting discussion of current events, you might ask, "Who do you suppose the *Tribune* reporter talked to in order to write the story about the winter ice rink at Wrigley, or the piece about the performance of schools in the city?" Or, upon reading a new poem, you might ask, "Why do you suppose the poet used actual quotes from other people when crafting this poem?" Or, I wonder why Katherine Applegate (2007), author of *Home of the Brave*, wrote, "When the flying boat, returns to earth at last . . ." (p. 3) instead of writing, "when the airplane finally lands." These questions and ponderings are designed to help readers see the thinking and experiences that inform and shape the texts they read. They are about helping kids understand that writers are real people, with real experiences, who have developed their own processes in writing that help them create the texts read by real people in the world—including in schools and classrooms.

Our thinking aloud and hypothesizing about possible decisions authors have made is one way to help young writers begin to see behind-the-scenes thinking. Another option is to turn to the authors themselves. Author and publisher websites and blogs, YouTube videos, and other technologies can help us easily connect with authors. In doing so, we can learn about the research and detective work that, for example, Kathleen Krull (http://www.youtube.com/watch?v=Fus1T6r6smc) and Kelly O'Connor McNees (http://kellyoconnormcnees.com/about-louisa-may-alcott) engage in as they write biographies or historical fiction novels, or learn more about why Monica Brown (http://www.monicabrown.net/about/index.html) publishes her work as bilingual texts and how she used people from her real life when writing her first piece of fiction, *Butterflies on Carmen Street* (2007).

Seeing the Thinking behind Peers' Texts

Although published pieces often offer important insights into writing and possible techniques, sometimes they are beyond our writers' current reach. However, peer work and peer thinking often provide perfect next steps that writers within a particular classroom might take. The following scenario is an example of how elementary writers might learn how to provide support and evidence for their thinking while composing essays—for themselves and others.

As Angel worked to develop his essay about the challenges of having younger siblings, he had some ideas about how he might provide evidence for his stance—including how his younger brother often got him in trouble by telling their mother that Angel either wasn't sharing his soccer ball or, worse yet, had kicked the ball too hard, both of which resulted in their mother yelling at Angel. After jotting down examples— evidence to support his first point—Angel moved on to his second point: that younger siblings wake others up in the middle of the night with their crying. He knew this often happened to him, but he didn't know if his own experience was enough evidence to convince his readers. In a conference, Angel easily identified his problem—he was stuck because he didn't have additional evidence. He wondered how he could provide research to support his position. Because this was one of the first times that Angel and his third- and fourth-grade classmates had written essays, extensive outside research was not a focal point of their study. However, gathering evidence was still possible. Soon, Angel and a classmate were moving about the room surveying their friends, recording on a notepad how many had younger siblings that woke them up at night with their crying. Very quickly Angel had the necessary data: twenty-three of the twenty-six students in Room 342 shared similar experiences. As writing time came to a close, Angel placed his data sheet on the ELMO document camera for all to see. He and his assisting classmate explained the problem they had encountered—not having enough evidence to support their idea—and they proceeded to share how they had solved the problem by gathering data. Together the class crafted one possible way that Angel could infuse the data into his writing. The notion of gathering information from classmates, family members, or others in the school seemed to be a welcome strategy, one that other classmates could use to help provide support for their own diverse essays about sibling rivalry, local gangs, and the importance of eyeglasses.

Scaffolding Reflections on Decisions Made

As teachers, we need to create supportive contexts, help make visible the decisions writers make as they compose, and support young people in taking a critical look at what they did, why they did it, and what they might do next. This section builds on the notion that young writers learn how to *see problems* as they write as well as learn *how to tackle* such challenges. It explores how we can zoom in on a particular aspect of writers' work to look more holistically at thinking and decision-making processes. Examples highlight how we can scaffold students' thinking as they work to make decisions and determine both what worked well for them and what may not be the most useful practices given the situation or who they are as writers.

Scaffolding Reflections on Decisions Made

- Zooming in: Reflecting on revision decisions

- Reflecting holistically on process

- Supporting collaborative work

- Making plans: Supporting alignment between intentions and actions

Zooming In: Reflecting on Revision Decisions

After several days during which mini-lessons focused on revision, young writers in a multi-age writing community were asked to think about the revision strategies they'd recently used. At the time, Maxwell and Carter were third graders and Gino a fifth grader in his second year of learning in English in the United States. When we look at their thinking, several points are worth noting (see Figure 4.4). As Maxwell literally cut apart a photocopy of his draft and reconfigured the order, he was thinking not only about what made sense to him but also about what might make sense to a reader. Revision for him was about making writing clear for the intended reader (as well as for the writer). So while Maxwell was thinking about how a particular strategy was working for him, he was also telling us about his understanding of why it's important to write well. In contrast, Carter identified multiple strategies. To add more description, he needed to take stock of "igzactly what I had" before new information could be added—for him, rewriting helped him do that. As a writer who struggles with motor skills, Carter found that rewriting or typing helped him to see what was already there and then think about where additions or deletions might occur. Carter's reflections also reveal that "adding more" could mean adding entirely new paragraphs to a particular piece, not just adding more words or a new line. Last, Gino saw his recent work as efforts to make his writing "make sense" to the person who reads (raid) it. Sentences were helping him organize his ideas and he, like Maxwell, knew that his readers needed those sentences to understand his thinking.

Asking these three boys to put their recent actions on paper lets us see what they did and why, but also calls on them, as they examine the *whys* behind their work, to articulate the decisions they had made. In these three cases, the strategies they selected seemed to suit their purposes; however, they also knew it was okay to admit when a strategy didn't work out as planned. Their classmate Amir demonstrated this even more clearly. He tried "changing genre" as a revision strategy, explaining that he tried "writing a poem from a story," but he ended up returning to the story because the poem left out some important parts and thus didn't work out very well. These writers knew that "stories of success" weren't necessary; rather, giving honest accounts of real writing challenges and attempts at problem solving were helpful because as writers they needed to know what worked for them, when it worked, when it might not, and why.

As I mentioned in the opening paragraph of the chapter, kids don't necessarily come to us explicitly thinking about their processes and decisions. These particular young people had a great deal of experience thinking about their decisions. Their teacher and classroom environment regularly called on them to do so.

Figure 4.4: Reflecting on revision decisions.

MAXWELL	CARTER	GINO (new ELL)
What is one revision strategy that you have used recently? *I have been using the cutting & posting stratagey (changing the order)*	What is one revision strategy that you have used recently? *① by adding more descriptive writing* How did it help you? *① wen for a start thinkirs about descriptions one mean anixelf new para graph in my Peace* *② re writirs it helped me figure out izgacty whay I had qnd gave me a new paragoughn it added some other descriptpns and gave me sonithim new to work with*	What is one revision strategy that you have used recently? *Well I revise and makes santeses* How did it help you? *Becase you revision to make santeses so the story raid makes suateses*
What is one revision strategy you've used recently? I have been using the cutting & pasting stratagey (changing the order). **How did it help you?** It helped me & hopefuly everyone else understand it more clearly.	**What is one revision strategy you've used recently?** (1) to adding more descriptive (2) rewriting **How did it help you?** (1) when for a start thinking about descriptions gave me an entirely new paragraph in my peace. (2) Rewriting it helped me figure otu izgzactly what I had and gave me a new paragraph it added some other descrptions and gave me something new to work with.	**What is one revision strategy you've used recently?** Well I revise and makes senteses. **How did it help you?** Becase you revision to make santeses so the story the you raid makes sense.

The kids featured in the next example have less experience with this sort of reflective thinking. They're all capable of coming to see, name, and assess their own decisions, but as their teachers know, this takes time and intentional invitations, feedback, and experience.

Reflecting Holistically on Process

Another way we can help kids see what they're doing in the process of constructing a particular piece of writing or exploring a particular line of thinking is to invite them to articulate and assess their process. When I was working with Jerri and her fifth-grade writers, we began by asking students to tell us about what they did when composing. Early in the year, they wrote things like the comments by Logan, Mark, Maeve, and Max in Figure 4.5.

In studying students' initial responses, we noted that their intentions focused on getting the process "right." In the weeks that followed, Jerri angled her teaching to turn students toward making more decisions on their own. Instead of assigning a topic or handing them a scoring guide, she asked them to write regularly in response to class mini-lessons. Once they had a collection of daily writing samples, Jerri asked the students to draw from their daily writings to craft a piece of their own choosing that demonstrated what they were learning about voice and the role of peer conversations while writing. Several months later, after they had published the piece of their own choosing, we asked the same writers similar questions, and this time found evidence that they were taking more ownership of their process and beginning to think about what worked for them and what they genuinely had done to craft their most recent pieces.

Logan: I thought of a movie I saw and changed the character. I thought of random things that should happen to him.

Mark: I saw lots of rooms [when touring the school] and the one room with the buttons so I thought of a robot. I had just read a book and the idea just kept coming and it goes like the book. [While drafting I thought] what would be interesting and wrote it and changed it—a lot of things. [When talking with my partner,] he said it was just like Goosebumps and that it gave a lot of detail. I thought I did get a good story; juicy details are what I could have done better.

Maeve: I looked around where I am and think what object would inspire me. [To help myself write the piece,] I stretched the truth and I asked my friends if they liked the idea. [While drafting] I would stop typing and think what's a better idea. [When talking with

Figure 4.5: Reflecting on process: Fifth-grade cases.

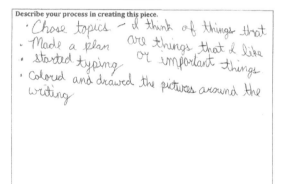

Logan

Describe your process in creating this piece.

rough draft
fixes it
final draph

Mark

Describe your process in creating this piece.

∘ I brainstormed about good thoughts to make my story sound good.
∘ I wrote a ruft draft to get the main Idea.
∘ I edited it and add new thoughts
∘ (will type it soon)
∘ (check again to make it Perfect)

Maeve

Describe your process in creating this piece.

∘ Chose topics — I think of things that are things that I like
∘ Made a plan or important things
∘ started typing
∘ Colored and drawed the pictures around the writing

Max

Describe your process in creating this piece.

∘ Planned it on a website
∘ Printed helpful chart
∘ Wote rough draft
∘ checked with teacher
∘ Wrote final coppy
∘ Turned it in

my partner, we had] a lot of misunderstanding in both our writings and we fixed a lot of commas. I think my weakest spot was the details, and I think my next time I write I could of figured out a better plot.

Max: We took a tour around the school to see what had happened and I stretched the truth. [When developing my piece,] I chose one of the events that happened [in our tour] and talked with Jay about my piece. I typed the whole piece and then reread it and revised. [When talking with my partner,] I read his story with lots of expression and gave him a lot of tips. I thought "oh my god this is such a great piece" but I could use a little more practice with organization.

Logan moved closer to knowing that the writing process isn't a three-step process that is the same for everyone. As a movie watcher, he was beginning to understand that he could use his experiences to inspire action-packed writing. Mark moved from believing in a linear process that ended with perfection to seeing that writing changes as one drafts and that, as a writer, his work can always be better, specifically with regard to details. Maeve moved from doing what she was told to doing what made sense to her. She consulted with friends even before her teacher conducted mini-lessons that invited kids to confer with peers. She was beginning to see that revision happens *while* drafting as she paused during her typing to think and rethink what might come next. Like Mark, Maeve thinks she has work to do as she continues to write, even though the particular piece she was reflecting on has already been published. And Max, who initially wrote about completing graphic organizers and transferring information to a draft, was beginning to see how he could turn experiences from his life into writing, and that peers could play a role in the development of his work.

While we can chart the students' growth through examples like these, we can also see opportunities for more thinking and teaching. Why, for example, does Max think he needs more practice with organization? What does he see in his piece that leads him to say it isn't organized well? And how does one go about gaining more experience in organizing writing? What might Maeve do to learn to gather and use information to create strong plots? And how might Logan learn to dig deeper into the nuances of his work so that he can identify more ways to plan the things that happened to his character? How can we help him see the differences between random and purposeful planning, especially how random successions of action impact the overall piece? What might he do in future writing to bring more cohesion to his work?

Taking the time to step back from our writing to consider the decisions we are making and how particular steps in our process are working out is one way to identify the decisions we've made. So too is engaging with others. Writers might find it helpful to talk with others about their writing work, as well as look back to see how their talk has influenced their piece and thinking as a writer. As teachers, we need to provide scaffolds so that productive conversations can happen in the moment as well as over time as writers learn what it means to think with and learn from other writers.

Supporting Collaborative Work

Whether working with primary- or intermediate-age writers, we cannot assume that merely putting them in groups or partnerships will lead to productive thinking about writing processes and practices. We often need to scaffold and teach young writers how to engage in productive conversation that can help them improve a particular piece as well as develop their thinking about the art of writing itself.

Recently, in a third-grade classroom where most students were nearing a point of publication, they used peer writing conferences as a means of improving their writing and their thinking about what it means to think like a writer. After a brief gathering of the whole class on the carpet to outline the range of activities that writers could be engaged in during writing time on that Wednesday, the teacher, Dena, called seven writers to the back table to talk as the rest of the class continued with their own writing work. These students had turned their writing in to her the day before because they were ready to talk about their pieces. Dena had read the pieces and provided one or two marginal comments for each writer to think more about. Although she could have provided additional comments for some of these pieces, she limited herself to one or two areas for the writers to think more about. She began the small-group table conversation by saying, "As I read, I had some questions that I want you to think about and work on." She then gave Julian his piece back and began a brief conversation with him as others at the table listened in.

Dena: Julian, I want you to think about two things when you reread it. Think about what parts need to be in the story. *[Pointing to one part in his piece]* Is this important for the reader to know to understand the story? And then I was confused about your ending; it seemed like you just stopped without finishing out your sentence or thinking. Okay? In a minute I'm going to ask you and Beto to go work and talk together.

Beto, look through yours and see if you might be able to find some places where you can do more revision. Adding more of your thoughts, your feelings, descriptions using your five senses. . . .

I want you two to go over to the carpet. Others, make sure you're listening because you're going to do this too. Start with Julian. Julian, read your piece to Beto. Beto, listen, see if you hear parts that are confusing or parts that Julian could clarify. And then switch. . . .

When the kids moved to the carpet, Julian read, and Beto looked over his shoulder reading. When he finished, Beto began:

Beto: What . . . *[pause]*

Julian: Which parts do you think are confusing?

Beto: *[pointing to a part in the text]* What's G-force?

> **Julian:** Do you want me to fix that? *[immediately, he adds more writing to his paper]* What else was confusing?

After continuing in this manner for a few minutes, the boys turned to Beto's paper, again as side-by-side readers.

> **Julian:** I thought that it was confusing that, what's that? *[pointing to the text]*
>
> **Beto:** *Celebration*, that it was a kind of party; it's what it say in the dictionary.
>
> **Julian:** *[going on in the discussion]* I thought it was confusing that you said you *buyed* a pen because it's not really a word, it's *bought*. Do you know how to write *bought*? Here, I can write it on this piece of paper." *[writes the word* bought *on a slip of paper]*

After both boys finished giving their own reactions, they turned to the feedback they'd recieved from their teacher. Beto, when referring to Dena's feedback, noted that he needed to "put more of [his] thoughts and [his] feeling in" his writing. The two began to pursue that work together.

> **Beto:** When I saw the bounce house.
>
> **Julian:** What?
>
> **Beto:** Bounce house, I was really happy.
>
> **Julian:** Bounce house; what did you do?
>
> **Beto:** I take off my shoes and run into the bounce house. . . .
>
> **Julian:** There are a couple more lines, you can write that, down here *[pointing to a part in Beto's piece]*
>
> **Beto:** There was a bounce house, and I took my shoes off and my brother saw me took off my shoes, he took off his too, and we ran to the bounce house.

As Beto began to add these lines to his piece, Julian told a short story about how his cousin too had been surprised by a bounce house.

This collaboration was one of the first times the kids in this classroom had paired with peers to talk about their writing and what they might do next. As Julian and Beto sat together on the carpet, they drew on several experiences to make their work together worthwhile. First, they began by using the structure that Dena explained to them in the small group. Less than a minute passed between hearing the instructions Dena gave them and the opportunity to talk with each other. Second, when Beto tried to remember what he was supposed to ask Julian, Julian assisted

Beto by restating the question, "What parts do you think are confusing?," reflecting Julian's additional experience working in English. Beto's pointing demonstrated that he knew where he wanted Julian to work more on his piece. When the boys had finished the first part of their conversation, they turned to their teacher's marginal comments that aligned with the personal feedback she had shared briefly with each writer at the back table. In Beto's case, she'd asked him to go back and find places for more revision—to add information. Beto began to tell Julian about the bounce house featured in his writing, stating that he was "really happy." Their subsequent talk led Beto to create a more detailed scene that better shared his excitement (when he and his brother quickly discarded shoes and raced into the bounce house). Julian then helped him find a place to insert those details, and the revision work continued.

Note that in this first attempt at peer writing work, although the kids are beginning to make decisions on their own, they're not left completely alone. Dena guided their start, the boys helped each other with procedure and language, and they used their teacher's notes to help them continue their work after they'd each taken an initial turn at sharing their pieces. When I think about this conference, it reminds me that as we begin to ask kids to talk with others, we need to think about how we can support them without making all of the decisions for them. We need to strike a balance between support and independence so that we don't make them rely completely on their own experiences and still expect productive work.

When Sylva, a teacher in another public school, asks her first and second graders to confer with one another, she uses a different mechanism for support—a video camera. One way she incorporates videos is in class mini-lessons focused on "how writers talk." Sylva uses the camera to document student-to-student interactions during their writing processes. She later invites class members to view the videos, focusing on what they see their peers doing and figuring out how they can name the ways in which partners are helping each other. She then asks kids to consider making similar productive moves in their own writing conferences. Sylva also uses videos after publication of writing. She asks kids to think back to "what helped you write this piece" and "who helped you" and "how they helped you." Together they view videos and focus on suggestions given by peers. They talk about final published pieces in which the results of peer suggestions are obvious, as well as those published pieces in which readers can't detect the influence of suggestions. And they learn that part of being a good writer is sorting through suggestions and deciding what changes best suit the work at hand, rather than just doing everything your friends and teacher might tell you to do. What matters are the reasons for making a change, the needs of the piece and situation, and the decisions made by the writer.

Sylva and Dena's scaffolds not only help writers work collaboratively but also make visible what writers might do en route to a finished work. It's important for young people to be familiar with a range of possible actions and decisions so that they can select just the right strategy to meet specific needs.

Making Plans: Supporting Alignment between Intentions and Actions

Supporting young people in their journey to become wise writers who can make and pursue their own plans means making sure they have experience in looking back at what they've done, as well as the ability to look forward and know what they might do next.

Before and During: Making, Carrying Out, and Revising Plans

Writers in Room 204 become well versed in stating their writing plans. Following the day's lesson and using a modified version of Nancie Atwell's (1987, 1998) Status of the Class chart, the teacher asks students to share what they will be working on during writing time. For example, after a lesson focused on ways in which writers balance narration and dialogue, several students stated that they were going to reread their work and think about when dialogue or narration is most appropriate. Because kids are always at different places in their writing work and have different needs, other kids shared plans that included "working on a title to help focus my piece" and "continuing to add internal monologue so you [readers] know what's going on in the narrator's mind." According to their teacher, the students needed to have plans. But she also knew that kids were at different places with their planning skills, so she often used conferences during workshop time as a way to check in on the kids and to see if the work they were doing matched their intended plans. Aware that writers often need to change their minds, she also knew that some students were less experienced with figuring out what they might do next. So conferences become a place where she could begin by asking, "What are you working on now?," following up with, "What did you say you were going to be working on today? Tell me why your original plans didn't work out," or "Tell me why what you're doing right now makes more sense," or "Given what you're doing today, what do you think your plans might be for tomorrow?" Little by little, with guidance, students became more experienced in making plans that actually worked. As the year went on, their writing work more often aligned with their vision and progress.

After Writing: Setting Goals and Deciding How to Meet Them

Another way to help young writers develop a sense of where they're going and how they might get there is by goal setting. When we ask young people to set goals, we can also ask them to think about what they might do to reach their goals. Often, when first asked to set goals, kids will say that their goal is to "write better"; when asked what they might do to learn to write better, "practice" is a common response. While we do learn to write by writing, we also need to challenge ourselves in specific ways, so teachers need to help students become more focused with their goals and the next steps they will take to achieve them. If we want students to make the connection between what we teach them and when in their real writing lives they might decide to use this teaching, associating goals with specific actions is important. Look at how a group of fifth-grade writers improved their goal setting. At the beginning of the year, we asked them to craft some initial goals for themselves, including potential steps they might take to achieve those goals. Figure 4.6 illustrates two goals, articulated by two individual writers in the class but representative of the class as a whole. While these goals demonstrate some good thinking on the part of these eleven-year-old writers, the actions they named to reach those goals weren't very specific. But we knew that with scaffolded instruction these students could learn to identify more useful and specific actions. One way to achieve this scaffolding is to ask questions. For example, after Mark states that he intends to improve his ability to "attract the reader," he elaborates that he's going to "make it creative and interesting." Our question to him became *how*: Is he going to insert research? Include dialogue? Insert more action-oriented scenes? Is he going to focus on language choice and make characters talk and act as they would in the real

Figure 4.6: Setting goals: First attempts.

Right now, what are your goal(s) for yourself as a writer? And, what can you do to help yourself reach your goal(s)?

Goal	What I can do to reach this goal
MARK To attract the reader	to make it creative and intresting
MAEVE To have more detail	To really think about the object your writing

world? Is he going to make lists of language associated with the topic and reread to find passages in which language can be altered?

In subsequent teaching, students were asked to think specifically about giving directions to someone (in this case, themselves) about what they could do to meet their goal. They were asked to reflect on specific strategies they had already explored as well as actions taken during their unit of study, and on how or when such strategies and actions might be useful in subsequent writing. On one occasion, as the class toured the school, they took notes on actual activity they noticed going on around them. Their teacher encouraged them to think about their tour not only as an experience designed for one day's worth of work in their writing curriculum, but also as the kind of "live activity" they might experience in other places, such as at home, in the park, on the train—all of which could become resources that could help them develop their writing.

Two months later, after publication of a piece of writing, students were asked to set new goals and intended actions. Figure 4.7 illustrates goals and intentions written by some of the students at this point in the class. This time, kids inched closer to (1) naming goals that matched their needs and (2) articulating actions they could intentionally pursue. Edwin's first goal and action, for example, are clearly aligned. Unlike the students in the first group of examples, Edwin wasn't going to be "more creative"; rather, he was going to conduct research by studying

---

Figure 4.7: Setting goals: Continued efforts.

Right now, what are your goal(s) for yourself as a writer? And, what can you do to help yourself reach your goal(s)?

Goal	What I can do to reach this goal
EDWIN My goal is to be more expressive in my writing	I can study peoples emotions and write them down
My goal is to make a vision in my readers mind.	I can make a drawing and describe it. Make and conversation
QUENTIN Dont quit something that you start writing	If you stop at a chapter, just write a little bit more so you don't forget what youre writing about.

how people express emotions. His plan to write down his observations provided him with real data he could then use in his writing—data that could lead to "more expressive" writing. Edwin's goal was aligned with his plans, and his plans were actions that he could actually pursue with clarity. The third goal comes from Quentin, someone who constantly writes at school and at home. At the time of writing this goal, he had an ongoing project that involved multiple chapters of text. Creating a long text was important to him at the time. Reading his work, we could see that making his ideas connect to one another was important for his readers. If we look at his intended actions, we see that he's not planning to stop at the end of one chapter, but instead intends to write a little more. This could help him remember where he's going and better connect his ideas—a plan that matches a true need in his work.

Just as kids need experience and guidance in making oral plans before independent writing time, they need scaffolding and experience to write appropriate goals with clear plans of action. Helping kids see the promise in their first attempts and then supporting them as they hone their goals to genuinely match their needs will help them develop productive writing lives that extend well beyond our time with them.

Engaging young writers in intentional decision making before, during, and after writing calls for shared visions of the work that writers engage with, including what constitutes quality writing, what it means to work with supportive writing communities, and what it means to choose processes, practices, and projects that work for an individual writer. It follows, then, that writers need experience in seeing decisions made, making their own decisions, and assessing the utility of each decision. This means that as teachers of young writers, we need to establish predictable practices by which kids come to know that they are going to be asked again and again to say what they did and why, and say what they are going to do and why. If writers are accustomed to turning in writing and waiting for someone else to tell them whether it's good or ineffective and what they did wrong, they'll need time and support to shift their thinking and practices. And if we want writers to own their processes and decisions, they need our intentional support and teaching to move them to places where they are writers with visions and missions.

Chapter Five

Teaching with Intention: Assessment as a Means to Understand Experiences and Pursue Next Steps

Previous chapters have emphasized that teachers and young writers need to have a vision for where they're going and plans for how they might pursue and realize their intentions. A real part of achieving any vision is knowing how you are doing along the way. In practice, this means periodically stopping to examine how you are progressing, because assessing progress is a regular part of learning. For example, as I improve my gardening skills, I'm constantly examining the status of my plants: watching them flourish, deciding on the right time to harvest, figuring out the best possible response to wilting plants and pests. I know there are "rules of thumb" to follow, but the condition of my backyard and the weather of a particular season also matter. I read, I consult with friends and neighborhood gardeners, I try what I think is best given my current understanding of the plant situation, and I watch my garden and adjust my activities in it with varying degrees of success and insight. Similarly, when I'm at the racetrack with my husband, Tim, I notice that he is constantly making changes to both his race car and his driving techniques. He gathers data in a more formal way than I do with my gardening because his dashboard electronically collects data about car temperature, speed, rotation, and so forth that he can download onto his computer for analysis, but he uses information in a similar way—to see what he's done well and where he can continue to improve. Tim's close tracking of his progress helps him not only think about what he might do next but also see his growth over time.

Think about your own experiences with gardening, racing, cooking, or some other pursuit. How do you gather information to get better at what you do? I think you'll agree: assessment is necessary for learning to garden well, race well, cook well, and to do lots of other things well—including writing.

Unfortunately, assessment has taken on different meanings given the times and contexts in which we teach. Assessment and accountability discourses have often led people to equate assessment with adequate yearly progress (AYP), levels, and a deficit perspective, in which the primary focus is on scores or what students are missing rather than on the skills and experiences they possess and that subsequently can be built on. While we can't ignore contextual conditions or challenges, we also can't ignore our professional knowledge and visions for writers.

Let's return to our visions for writers and writing instruction. Look at what you wrote in Chapter 1 for Invitations 1.1–1.3 regarding your vision for writing, writers, and writing instruction; your classroom practices; and the sources that inform and shape your thinking. Given what you believe right now (which may or may not exactly match your thinking when you read Chapter 1), what might you say about your vision for assessment that aligns with your belief system (see Invitation 5.1)?

Invitation 5.1: Articulating a Vision for Assessment: What You Think Right Now

Revisit your vision for writing, writers, and writing instruction. *Given this vision, this is what I believe right now about assessment:*

Articulating a vision for assessment can be challenging, especially as assessment can so easily become focused on the most accessible aspects of writing. Looking at the conventions of actual words on the page is often the dimension of writing assessment with which we're most familiar, and perhaps most comfortable. However, if our vision for writers involves introducing students to flexible practices that are then their responsibility to refine and revise in order to meet the needs of particular situations, then both our formative and summative forms of assessment should match our beliefs. Furthermore, if our vision includes student self-sufficiency and the ability to make decisions beyond our watch, then young writers must develop understandings of their own processes and we, as their teachers, must know what they're doing and thinking as they select ideas, collect information, reflect on life, develop their work, get themselves going, keep themselves on task or get themselves back on track, organize their work, start over, and so on. This expanded notion of assessment is more difficult work because we're not working just with words frozen in final drafts, but instead with active writers whose thinking processes and practices are embedded in the lively interactions and activities of everyday classroom life. How then might we wrap our minds around what young people are thinking and doing so that we can provide just the right feedback and appropriate teaching for the writers and the situation? How can our vision for assessment match our commitment to helping young people become writers who can make decisions amidst changing communicative demands and rhetorical conditions? How can we ensure that assessment feedback genuinely attends to how students are doing throughout the writing process, provides useful advice for further growth, and responds to how well writers are meeting their goals?

Just as our vision for writers is not an individual invention, neither is our thinking about assessment. While educational policy—at federal, state, and local levels, which includes policies in our school buildings—may be a strong influence on our definition of assessment, many other resources and lines of thinking can contribute to productive understandings of what assessment is and can be in our teaching and learning lives. Drawing from professional organizations, colleagues, researchers, and teachers I know, I see assessment as part of a larger process of learning that draws on the right tools and practices (e.g., self-assessments, rubrics, feedback, guided observations, reflection) at the right times to facilitate continuous learning—by both students and teachers. In my vision, assessment is a collaborative and malleable process that transpires over time. It's not a one-way street with experts, internal or external, passing down information that tells a student where he or she stands; rather, assessment encompasses specific feedback that enables improvement that can be shared amongst a community of writers. Assessment is flexible and designed to capture, and help teachers and students understand and act on, the rich information embedded in the diverse language experiences that young people bring with them into classrooms. Because there is a fruitful relationship between interest, challenge, and performance, assessment, I believe, ought to be aligned with our curriculum—without simplifying the curriculum, as far too many assessments do. Effective assessment means intimately knowing the ins and outs of the art of writing, which often means that teachers too need regular opportunities to develop an understanding of and reflect on what they're looking at and looking for as they endeavor to best support young writers. And finally, assessment is about balance. It involves taking the time to collect and analyze information to shape just the right instruction without letting collection and analysis dominate teaching and learning time: students must have ample opportunities to try out and take on new practices and new ways of being writers.

This is my vision, one that has been developed through years of experience with writers in classrooms and through my reading and reflecting on the experiences of many other teachers and researchers (Anderson, 2005; Darling-Hammond, 2010; NCTE/IRA Joint Task Force, 2010; NCTE, 2007). And I urge all of you to think hard about your own visions, in part because if we as teachers want to (re) claim assessment as a useful tool in developing writers who understand and use the power of writing to shape their lives, we must develop instruction and teach with a clear vision of the possibilities and promises of what assessment can be.

In many ways, this chapter extends the thinking expressed in Chapter 4. Here, however, I officially use the word *assessment* as a means of reclaiming the term and recognizing that when we help kids see and reflect on their actions as writers, we're really helping them assess their growth through the products they create and the processes they engage with. In this chapter, I begin with a vision of what assessment is about and for, as a way to guide an exploration of how formative and summative tools and practices might be used individually and collaboratively to determine what writers already know and need, and the ways in which they progress within particular time frames. And, as in Chapters 3 and 4, visions are paired with actual decisions made by teachers intentionally working to use assessment as a tool for learning.

Moving from Our Own Vision to Shared Visions: Creating a Shared Vision

Our assessment visions and decisions are a reflection of what we value. While we may draw on our own professional experiences of attending conferences, reading professional materials, and talking with team members to create our own vision for assessment, if we want to focus on who our students become as writers, we need a vision that extends beyond our students' time in one classroom. We need to reach out to colleagues, talk about our vision, and make some shared decisions. This doesn't mean becoming carbon copies or clones of one another or scripting all that we do, but it does mean getting on the same "big page," where there is space for both individual ingenuity and continuity for young people. Although this might unfold in many different ways, consider as you read the following scenarios how two sites are working to build shared visions and possibilities for the writers in their care.

As a school-based literacy coach, Shirley has many responsibilities as well as many opportunities to help create shared visions, as well as complementary, cohesive practices, amongst a diverse staff of approximately thirty-four preK–8 public school teachers. Early in the school year, Shirley and the staff held a series of elective, informal, before- and after- school sessions related to writing and writing workshops. One particular series of conversations focused on assessment and how, as grade-level teams and a school, they wanted to track and communicate writers' work. As small groups of faculty gathered in study group–like conversations, they shared past practices related to assessment, perused resources that offered different frameworks and practices, and started sharing their thinking about the need to move "beyond pieces" in their assessment practices. Through their dialogue, it became clear that they valued their students' development of writing practices and processes that enabled students, over time and experience, to engage in writing work without teacher guidance. They envisioned students becoming people who can persevere through challenging writing endeavors, people who can decide when and where revision is needed, people who can decide when and what kind of writing might accomplish lifework in their communities. Therefore, teachers needed assessment tools and practices that would support them in this work. They looked at observational checklists they might tweak to align with their vision, discussed how they could communicate progress with students about non-print-based dimensions of writing, and debated how these dimensions of writers' work might be reflected in the current grading structure and system. While teachers didn't arrive at *the* answer, they came up with possibilities to pursue, some of which are featured in this chapter.

Across the city, another team of teachers convened during the summer to think about their visions—individual and shared—about writing and assessing writers and writing over time. Chris, Katie, Katie, and Jacque (grades 4–8 teachers) shared the same students over time and came together with an awareness that the ways in which writing and writing instruction transpired in their classrooms were informed by their somewhat varied visions. Knowing that a shared vision of success over time was best for students in their collective care, they met to discuss their current thinking about the features of quality writing and what they knew about their writers. If kids were to progress from year to year in their ability to craft quality pieces that accomplished diverse ends, how would these teachers define *quality*? This was the first question they needed to tackle. They began their work by agreeing to use categories that identified features of writing that, from their perspectives, were important elements of quality writing. They decided to focus initially on ideas and content, organization, structure and form, voice, language, and conventions. Together these teachers created initial descriptors for four degrees of understanding and development in each focal area. Then, using the same structure, they created additional rubrics with increased expectations for each of the core categories. Rather than creating a"fourth-grade rubric" and a"fifth-grade rubric," however, they designed three anchor rubrics to be used in an overlapping manner across their students' years in their school (see Figure 5.1).

These anchor rubrics articulated baseline expectations for writers as they progressed through their years at this school. Teachers, however, were welcome (and encouraged) to modify rubrics to fit particular units of study and writers' needs. For example, teachers could revise rubrics with students to reflect particular concepts studied, such as stanzas in poetry, or thesis statements in essays, or ways to infuse interview data into writing. Figure 5.2 includes this team's initial attempts to flesh out Writing Rubrics I and II.

Time, use, feedback, and reflection are likely to influence the continued development of these teachers' tools and shared practices. Articulating and using rubrics in this way—to connect expectations for both students and teachers across grade levels—invited conversations about how diverse writers define and engage in writing. This approach also made visible, for teachers, writers, and families, the minimum competencies writers should take ownership of as they wrote for a variety of purposes across the years.

Figure 5.1: Using shared rubrics across the years.

Rubric I	4th grade
	First semester 5th grade
Rubric II	Second semester 5th grade
	6th grade
	First semester 7th grade
Rubric III	Second semester 7th grade
	8th grade year

Figure 5.2: Creating a shared vision for writing assessment: Initial thinking—Rubric I and Rubric II.

Writing Rubric I

Student :_____   Date: _____

	4	3	2	1	Comments
Ideas and Content (Std. 6.2)	The topic and main ideas are clear, and the ideas are supported by several details (i.e. facts, similes, metaphors, or comparisons).	The topic and ideas are clear, and there are some important details that support the main idea.	The topic and ideas are somewhat clear, but important details to support the main ideas are missing.	The topic and ideas are unclear. It's hard to tell which information is most important. May be repetitious or disconnected thoughts with no main idea.	
Organization (Std. 6.2)	The writing has a catchy beginning to grab the reader's attention, a developed middle, and meaningful ending. The order of ideas makes sense. Transitions show how ideas connect.	The writing has a clear beginning, middle, and end. The order makes sense. There are some transitional words or phrases.	The writing attempts to have an introduction and/or conclusion, but they need more development. Some ideas seem out of order. Few transitions are used.	There is no real introduction or conclusion. The ideas are out of order and it is difficult for the reader to understand.	
Structure and Form (Std. 6.1)	Paragraphs are properly indented and begin in the correct places (when a new person is talking or there is a new idea or setting).	Paragraphs are indented; some begin when a new idea or setting is introduced or when a new person is talking.	Paragraphs are indented but many seem to be random breaks.	The writing is one long paragraph.	
Voice (Std. 6.3)	The writing has personality. The writer cares about the topic and speaks right to the reader.	The writing sometimes demonstrates care or enthusiasm for the topic.	The author's voice comes through in a few places.	The writing is bland or sounds like the writer is annoyed or doesn't like the topic.	
Language Choice (Std. 6.3)	Uses words and phrases that help create a picture in the reader's mind. May include five senses words.	Words and phrases are ordinary, with some attempt to create a picture in the reader's mind.	Words used are ordinary and the picture in the reader's mind is unclear.	The same words are used over and over, and some are used incorrectly.	
Conventions (Std. 6.4)	Few, if any, errors in spelling, punctuation, capitalization, grammar.	Spelling, punctuation and capitalization are usually correct, but there are some grammar problems.	Errors are frequent enough to make the writing difficult to understand.	Errors are so frequent they are distracting and make the paper difficult to read.	

Writing Rubric II

Student _____   Assignment _____

	4	3	2	1	0
Ideas and Content (Std. 6.2)	The topic and main ideas are clear. Details (i.e. facts, similes, metaphors, or comparisons) support the ideas.	The topic and ideas are clear, but there is not enough detail. The writing stays on topic but doesn't address minor parts of the assignment.	There is a very general topic, but the writing strays off topic or doesn't address major parts of the assignment.	The topic and ideas are unclear. It's hard to tell which information is most important. May be repetitious or disconnected thoughts with no main idea.	
Organization (Std. 6.2)	The writing has a catchy beginning to grab the reader's attention, a developed middle, and meaningful ending. The order of ideas makes sense. Transitions show how ideas connect.	The paper has a beginning, middle, and end. The order makes sense. Transitions are used, but some don't work well.	The paper has an attempt at an intro and conclusion. Some ideas seem out of order. Transitions need a lot of work.	There is no real introduction or conclusion. The ideas seem strung together in a loose fashion.	
Structure and Form (Std. 6.1)	Sentences are clear and complete. Some are longer than others. They begin in different ways. Paragraphs are properly indented and begin in the right spots. Each has one topic and has topic supporting, and closing sentences	Sentences usually complete. Some variety in beginning and length. Paragraphs are indented; some begin in the right spots and have topic supporting, and closing sentences.	Many poor constructed sentences. Little variety in beginning or length. Paragraphs often begin in the wrong places; may not have topic sentences.	The paper is hard to read because of incomplete, run-on, and awkward sentences. There is either one long paragraph or random breaks in paragraphs.	
Voice (Std. 6.3)	The writing has personality. The writer cares about the topic and speaks right to the reader.	The writing seems sincere, but the author's personality fades out.	The paper could have been written by anyone. The writing hides in the writing.	The writing is bland or sounds like the writer is annoyed or doesn't like the topic.	
Language Choice (Std. 6.3)	Uses vivid words and phrases that help make the meaning clear. May include 5 senses words	Words are ordinary, with a few attempts at descriptive words.	Words used are ordinary but generally correct.	The same words are used over and over, some incorrectly.	
Conventions (Std. 6.4)	Few, if any, errors in spelling, punctuation, capitalization, grammar	Spelling, punctuation and caps usually correct. Some grammar problems.	Errors are frequent enough to make the writing hard to understand.	Errors are so frequent they are distracting. The paper is almost impossible to read.	

Actions taken by both teams illustrate the centrality of vision in the assessment process—having concrete examples of the conviction that before we can assess degrees of progress and needs for support we need to know what we're looking at and for. And, when our focus is on how young people become writers and decision makers over time, we need to collaborate with colleagues to negotiate shared values so that we make decisions in light of students' overall experiences and learning trajectories. Remember that shared visions or values do not mean that classrooms are mirror images of one another; rather, shared visions mean that the core of "what matters most" is continuous over time. Developing shared visions about assessment is about taking ownership of assessment and doing, at any particular point in time, what educators think is next and best for their students. For example, in the case of Shirley's school, teachers shared a belief that learning to write well was about more than print on the page or conventional spelling. Once we have in mind that big picture we're aiming for, we can begin to investigate what writers know and need, as well as monitor their progress.

As you read the following sections that explore how we can learn what writers know and need, study how such practices support articulating where writers currently stand and how they're growing over time. Think about the featured teachers' visions for writing, writers, writing instruction, and assessment. Think about your own visions and subsequent practices. And then consider how these teachers' thinking and actions relate to the challenges, needs, and possibilities in your teaching and learning context.

Discovering What Writers Know and Need

As we work in learning communities where the focus is on becoming writers, we need to develop ways of seeing what kids know and need, as well as what we know and need. While we might go about this work in many different ways, this section explores the role of *on-demand* writing assessment practices and possibilities, the role of *observation* in coming to know and act on learner needs, and the role of *student reflections and rubrics* for learning.

Discovering What Writers Know and Need

- Using "on-demand" assessment for learning

- Using observations as assessment for learning

- Using student reflections and rubrics as assessment for learning

Using "On-Demand" Assessment for Learning

If we want to construct a class or grade-level picture of what our students already know so that we can craft subsequent instruction, we might engage students in a brief "on-demand" writing piece. Initially, this may make some readers cringe because of the way prompted writing as been constructed as a testing practice in which particular prescribed features are expected and dictated topics influence what writers have to say (or not say). Furthermore, we might equate such an experience with assigning fixed ratings that mark student performance and influence their identities as writers. Put that thinking aside for a moment. The on-demand writing I'm talking about is formative—it's designed for teachers to see what kids already know and where the edges are in their current knowledge. Then it's our job, using information that we glean from this kind of assessment, to tailor curriculum to the young people learning in our classrooms.

In one school where I worked, the teachers across a grade level asked their students, before beginning a personal narrative unit of study, to write a personal narrative about something from their lives. Students were asked to get as far as they could within the given time frame (in this case, one thirty-minute writing period) and to use what they knew about writing to write the best they could. Later, as a grade-level team, teachers used both observational checklist data and the actual pieces of student writing to determine what writers knew at that point in time and to begin thinking about what should come next for this particular group. As teachers examined the student writing, they sorted the narratives into four piles, from least to most developed. It's important to note that this sorting was a quick-and-dirty process, involving neither strict criteria nor hours of pondering. Nor were the piles created as a way to rank or label kids; rather, they were one small way to help teachers understand the range of experiences represented in their classrooms. They engaged in what Lucy Spence (2010) would call a generous reading—focusing on what the children *can do*. Once the four piles were complete, teachers examined each pile and made lists of what writers in each category could do. They paid attention to what students already knew about writing in general and, in this case, what they knew about personal narratives. The next list they developed focused on writers' needs, framed as potential next steps. Using a simple grid to make their notes (see Figure 5.3), they easily identified the kinds of teaching that the whole class needed, as well as more focused teaching needs for small groups.

Figure 5.3: Making notes: Writers' assets and next steps.

	I	II	III	IV
What writers can do				
Next steps				

Looking across charts also provided insights for continued teacher growth. When we looked closely at our initial assessments of strengths and decisions for next steps, patterns immediately emerged. Initial teacher observations regarding what the youngest primary writers could do and subsequently needed focused on concepts of print (e.g., directionality; use of image, text, and labels for meaning making), conventions (e.g., uses capitals/lowercase, spells own name conventionally, uses spaces), writerly habits and behaviors (e.g., writes independently, takes risks when spelling words), and developing content (e.g., details, elaborated ideas). This process of analysis—and analysis of the analysis—not only resulted in teachers adapting curriculum that was well suited to the actual learners in a given classroom but also challenged participants to continue to think about what skills and practices writers need to develop across time and experiences (see Figure 5.4).

Looking at actual pieces of writing and examining the focus of initial analysis is helpful in developing understandings of what both teachers and students know best and what they still need to know. However, if we also value those decisions learners make en route to putting words on the page or screen, we need tools and practices that allow us to capture the processes that writers engage in as they work.

Figure 5.4: Analysis of analysis: Examining what writers know and need.

Key: Know NEED	Emergent writer: Concept of Writing (pictures, text, …)	Meaning (point, reason for writing)	Form (b/m/e; similar ideas together) & Structure (treatment of subject/ focus; have a msg and stay with it)	Language (word choice)	Voice (sounds like writer)	Elaboration-Development (scenes, amt of detail, character traits, setting…)	Conventions	Habits
Observations of primary writing work	Writing and pictures convey meaning		Step-by-step stories About one topic STRETCHING OUT AN IDEA STAYING WITH BIG IDEA OR MOMENT			Some feelings/ emotions included CREATING DETAILED PICTURES & STORIES	Capitals USING PERIODS, SPACING DEVELOPING STRATEGIES FOR FIGURING OUT UNKNOWN WORDS	Choosing ideas DEVELOPING STAMINA

Using Observations as Assessment for Learning

For us, as teachers, to decide what kids need, we need to develop ways of seeing what they already know about the specifics of writing: a particular genre, writing processes, qualities of good writing, etc. This means looking at the writing they produce, as well as *how* they produce those pieces. To capture live classroom activity, engaging in ongoing observations of our students through keen kid-watching (Owocki & Goodman, 2002) can serve us well. As we examine student work, however, we need to think about what we're looking for and how we look, including what lenses we're using to observe, what we write down, and how we use this information to inform our next steps or decisions. In the interest of collecting useful and organized data, checklists or structures for focused notes often help teachers make the necessary connections between what is produced and how students produce it—in other words, finding ways to understand the kinds of writerly behaviors emphasized in this book.

To design a checklist that best fits the needs of the writers in our classrooms, we first need to articulate valued practices. Given the many useful practices that writers can take on over time, we might start with focused checklists that align with students' current needs and our current teaching. For example, one practice we might consider important is developing independence in student writers. If we consider how this practice might develop across years, teaching, and experience, our expectations might be aligned with the criteria articulated in Figure 5.5. Based on our beliefs about the role of independence, we could track students' actions on a class checklist, literally checking the category that best describes our observations on a given date, or we might include more specific data, in this case the approximate amount of time writers seem to be engaged in meaningful writing work: writing, reading, writerly talk, etc. (see Figure 5.6). In addition to valuing writers' stamina and good use of writing time, we might create a checklist that measures how writers encode ideas—do they write ideas "the best they can"; do they draw on multiple spelling strategies to help get their ideas into print; do they focus on content and clarity without getting hung up on achieving complete spelling accuracy?

Figure 5.5: Example writing practice.

	Primary ➤		Intermediate
A focus on writers' practices: *Working toward independence*	Develops stamina and perseverance during independent writing time by attending to writing work for increased periods of time	Practices independence and stamina by sticking with an idea/project over time and naming the writing work they will attend to on any given day	Uses writing time well and self-directs next steps in writing work by identifying needs and making decisions about how to attend to difficulties in physical writing work

Figure 5.6: Noting practices: A possible checklist.

Students	Date: October 3 Length of independent writing time: __20__ minutes				Date: October 10 Length of independent writing time: __25__ minutes			
	Engages in minimal writing work during writing time	Engages in writing work for less than half of writing time	Engages in writing work for most of writing time	Engages in writing work for full writing time	Engages in minimal writing work during writing time	Engages in writing work for less than half of writing time	Engages in writing work for most of writing time	Engages in writing work for full writing time
Alexis			✔				~22	
Jalessa		✔					~18	
Martin				✔				25

Or we might be interested in how writers talk—do they use storytelling to help develop their ideas; can they differentiate between social chatting and productive talk; do they turn to peers or the teacher when they encounter difficulty; do they specify what they need help with or just say "I'm stuck"; do they provide appropriate feedback? How writers use their time, how they get their ideas down in concrete form, and how they talk are all practices we might value. Checklists like these are a way to remind us of what we value, and they allow us to track students' engagement with such practices consistently so that we can see areas of growth and need.

Checklists are often quick and easy to complete, based as they are on broadscale observations of our students as they engage with writing work, but we may need more specific information to help us understand what kids know about particular processes and practices. If, for example, we're focused on how students generate ideas and how they get going in their writing work, we might first define for ourselves and for our students what we, as a classroom community, know about the ways in which writers generate ideas (see Figure 5.7). Then, rather than taking open-ended notes, we can focus our observations on particular dimensions of writerly processes, in this case how writers get started. We might create focused notes pages for ourselves that include all of our students' names listed in one column, space for notes in another, and the focus of our observations at the top of the page (see Figure 5.8). Given this information about what students know about productive writing practice, we need to make sure that our students have time to talk as they begin new pieces, especially if we've taught them to tell stories as a means of getting into writing stories.

Taking Notes, Using Notes: A Possible Approach

Anecdotal notes are a useful resource for reflecting on teaching and learning over time. Just taking notes, however, doesn't necessarily ensure that we can use the notes as a means to inform our next steps. We need a system or approach to note taking that best suits us and allows us to easily see and use information gathered. One elementary teacher and I who regularly conferred with writers in the same classroom decided to create a weekly notes page template that we could copy and use to think about in-the-moment teaching as well as learning over time. Here are the decisions we made when constructing our notes page template:

1. *Consider the information to be gathered.* We wanted to note how writers talked about their current work and needs, as well as capture the teaching that transpired within a particular interaction with a child on a given date.

2. *Design a format that allows for easy daily use as well as long-term use.* For us this meant making a one-page (front to back) form with a three-column table that included a row for each child in the class plus a few blank rows.

Student	Teaching and Learning Focus	Notes

We typed student names in the left-hand column so that notes about a particular student were always in the same location. The right-hand column was the biggest, the place where we took open-ended notes about how writers talked about their work, discussed their challenges, asked for help, etc. So as we listened and talked with students, we made notes in the right-hand column. After each conversation, we paused briefly to fill out the middle column, a space in which to record the focus of teaching and learning within a particular conversation. Because the space was small, we were reminded that the focus of a conversation also needed to be small. This helped us remember not to tackle everything a writer needed but rather to focus on a point or two that seemed most significant.

3. *Develop a practice for using the notes page.* For us this meant photocopying the form and, at the beginning of each week, attaching a clean copy of the form to clipboards, one for each of us. As we conferred with kids, we took notes and named the teaching that transpired. Each day we were able to see which students we'd not yet talked with. Ideally, we wanted to see each child at least once a week, but our system allowed us to be flexible too. The blank rows created space for returning to a particular child—especially in cases where we thought checking back in soon would be important. At the end of each week, we put our notes in a ring binder. Reviewing student progress over time was easy; all of the notes about one child were located in the same place, and we could thumb from page to page and examine both the student's and our actions over time.

Figure 5.7: Articulating guidelines for narrative notes.

A focus on process: Generating ideas and getting started	• Uses experiences, pictures, talk, reading, previous writing, and/or outside resources as tools to generate writing ideas • Uses a variety of strategies ranging from list making to freewriting to get started in writing work

---

Figure 5.8: Taking notes.

Week of: September 15	
FOCUS: Generating ideas and getting started	
Alexis	9/17 Uses photo taped on front of writing notebook to start his entry about sharks.
Jalessa	9/15 Starts writing using story she told to partner during think-pair-share, part of today's mini-lesson.
Martin	9/15 Needs a conference to get going today, decides to reread yesterday's writing for inspiration. After rereading opts to write about something that happened in his neighborhood last night, as the word *neighborhood* appeared in previous day's work.

Using Student Reflections and Rubrics as Assessment for Learning

Just as we can analyze student work and study student activity, so too can (and should) students. Izzy and her classmates' experiences with self-reflection and rubrics provide another window into what we can learn when we make learners' thinking integral to our assessment processes.

When fourth grader Izzy and her classmates began to formally study and write poetry, a primary focus of their study was the ideas that poets pursue. Students engaged in explorations and curricular conversations about what poets hope to accomplish through their writing and the range of issues and topics they pursue. Students explored the language used in poetry and the role of poetic devices such as similes, metaphors, and personification in accomplishing their own poetry-writing goals. And, last, they spent some time thinking about the role of punctuation and editing in guiding the reader through their poetry. What each writer did was also informed by his or her previous experiences with poetry (including weekly poetry pal sessions with second-grade learning buddies and daily classroom poetry reading and response experiences during morning routine).

Throughout this unit, these young poets were asked to self-assess their experiences and learning, using a narrative self-reflection form so that they could demonstrate through their own words what they had learned. Figure 5.9 illustrates some questions posed and a sampling of student responses.

Next, students were asked to evaluate their poems using a rubric. Many of us are well versed in using rubrics as tools to assess student work in subjective, yet fairly transparent and consistent ways. We know that rubrics help make visible the criteria to be assessed, as well as the characteristics that may accompany various degrees of performance.

While the foci of this unit were guided by what the students already knew about poetry, their teacher aligned student needs with state standards as a way of meeting both student needs and external goals. For example, Izzy's teacher constructed a rubric with the main areas of focus—meaning, poetic devices, word choice, and editing—along one axis and the degrees of accomplishment—exceptional, masters, progressing, below—along the other. She provided a brief narrative for each degree of accomplishment, attempting to make distinctions between the degrees of development. Knowing that the rubric was more than a tool for determining a grade (and I would argue that this is the key to honest assessment), Izzy and her classmates used the tool to examine their own poetry.

Some of Izzy's classmates were easily able to match their work with the characteristics described; some had infused new words and language into their work, others had tried to create images in readers' minds through the use of familiar comparisons, and so on. In Izzy's case, her work didn't fit the rubric characteristics well, yet she knew she had paid attention to class conversations and that she under-

---

Figure 5.9: Self-assessing experiences and learning: Narrative reflection form.

What was the hardest thing about writing poetry?

Finding the right topic to write about and finding the right words to say about the topic.

What was your favorite part about writing poetry?

I liked that we had to be creative and think of our own metaphors and similes. When I read a poem with a good metaphor, I think that's such a great and thoughtful metaphor.

Look back at the poems we read in class. What was your favorite poem or poet and why?

—One of my favorite poets is Walter Dean Myers because he uses juicy words, I think his poems are unique and have a deep meaning.

—One of my favorite poets is Langston huges because his poems are little battles against racism.

What do you know about poetry that you did not know before?

—I know a lot more poetic devices and different kinds of poems.

—I know that poetry can be anyway you want it to be.

stood the potential of things like figurative language (see Figure 5.10). But in the case of her poem titled "So What," such descriptions didn't fit her intentions. Izzy wrote "So What" as a simple poem in response to environmental concerns. She spoke directly to readers and wanted to convey the clear, direct message that soon enough, if not now, environmental issues will impact their lives. When faced with her poem and the rubric, Izzy matched her piece with the characteristics while adding commentary that illustrated her understanding of the core concepts through her explanation of why they were excluded from her work.

In this case, the rubric was not the only tool used for assessment. The process of self-assessment through both a rubric and narrative reflection allowed these young poets to see what they'd done (and not done) as well as articulate the reasoning behind decisions. In Izzy's case, she read her poetry, wrote about significant insights from the unit, made rating decisions, and added commentary in the margins, all of which allowed her teacher to see what Izzy understood about their study of poetry. The rubrics and her teacher's ongoing evaluation through conferences and observation led to a strong evaluation of Izzy's work and thinking. Izzy's teacher didn't simply add up the numbers on the rubric according to Izzy's self-scoring, but instead took into account the clear case Izzy made for why she did what she did and how she needed to modify the rubric criteria to suit her thinking and decision-making processes.

Although rubrics can be constructed to describe and evaluate the specific areas of intended learning within a unit of study, as Izzy cautions us, *how* we use them matters. We don't want to lock writers into following recipes but instead encourage them to make intentional and explicit decisions. We want assessment to genuinely show what writers know, and we must use that knowledge with intentionality as we plan and enact future instruction. In addition to asking students to use rubrics, giving them a chance to talk more fully about why they've made certain decisions about their writing helps support a kind of assessment that is much fuller than relying on a rubric alone.

Studying and Supporting Writers' Growth over Time

The ways in which I've discussed on-demand assessment, observations, and self-reflections and rubrics thus far present them as tools that shed light on what writers know at particular points in time. However, they, along with other practices, also can be used to show growth *over* time. We could, for example, make brief on-demand experiences a regular preassessment practice when we're studying a particular genre by asking students to show us what they currently know. Or we could

Studying and Supporting Writers' Growth over Time

- Monitoring progress and assessing actions

- Using feedback for growth

Figure 5.10: So what: Modifying criteria to match intentions and thinking.

So what

So what if all the
Dangers
to the world
don't aim directly at
you
they'll get to
you
soon enough

Rubric for Poetry Unit of Study

Title of Poem: So what

Name of Author: Izzy

I don't Know how to grade myself

Criteria	4- Exceptional	3- Masters	2-Progressing	1- Below
Meaning (Standard 2.A.3a)	Poem includes figurative language to make a powerful, clear picture in the reader's head	Poem includes figurative language to make a clear picture in the reader's head	Poem attempts to use figurative language	Poem lacks clear meaning
Poetic Devices (Standard 2.A.3c)	Poem successfully demonstrates an understanding of the poetic devices (simile, metaphor, personification, repetition, alliteration, etc.)	Poem demonstrates an understanding of the poetic devices	Poem demonstrates an attempt to use poetic devices	Poem does not use poetic devices
Word Choice (3.B.3b)	Poem includes many juicy words	Poem includes some juicy words	Poem includes one juicy word	Poem does not include juicy words
Editing (3.B.2d)	Poem demonstrates evidence of editing (spelling, capitalization, title, punctuation)	Poem demonstrates some evidence of editing	Poem demonstrates little evidence of editing	Poem demonstrates no evidence of editing

I don't think it's to say this is below some poems could not have juicy words and still be good

decide to design our anecdotal record-keeping system (see sidebar on page 103) as an easy way to trace interactions with and observations of a particular writer. Or we might use a portfolio as a place to keep not only more formal student writing but also their reflections and self-evaluations. We might also consider engaging students in their own ongoing analysis of their work, as well as the work of their peers, always making sure feedback is kind, critical, and instructive.

Monitoring Progress and Assessing Actions

If we want young people to see what they're doing as they write, we might ask them to reflect on and record their processes of creating a particular piece, as Maeve, Mark, Max, Logan, and their classmates were asked to do (see Chapter 4). We have other options, too. We can ask kids to keep track of their writing processes on a daily basis. To do this, you might ask students to use a T-chart and keep it in their writing notebook or writing folder to record the work they've done on each date. On each new day, ask them to revisit yesterday's actions and accomplishments when deciding on the new day's work (see Figure 5.11). Or we might ask them to use the "track changes" feature of word-processesing software as they revise. Using this feature and saving documents with the date as part of the file name (e.g., Article draft 2.16.10.doc, Article draft 2.19.10.doc) allows students (and us) to see and review the changes, progress, growth, or areas of need that unfold over time. We might, for example, find that some writers merely add more text at the end of their pieces. These writers may need instruction related to how and why writers dig into internal parts of their pieces to add, delete, or modify information. We might find writers who make very few changes in their work across many days. These writers might be starting their writing each day without rereading their work. Perhaps these writers don't yet understand the possible roles rereading their work can play in the writing process. Having a visual map like the T-chart or the visual trail of a writer's thinking can help writers and their teacher think and talk about previous decisions made and possible paths to pave in the days, weeks, units, and writing to come. Or we might engage writers in more formal coding and analysis of their work, as middle-grades teacher Renee has done with her students.

Renee is not a teacher who collects student writing, evaluates the work by some known or unknown criteria, and returns the work with a circled grade or number; she turns the work of analysis over to her students. Both during and at the end of units of study, she distributes a coding sheet and a rubber-banded set of colored pencils to writers, asking them to use the codes to mark particular features or lines of thinking in their papers. She might ask them to place blue stars at the beginning of each new paragraph, thus making visible students' understanding of the presence or absence of paragraphing in their piece, or she might ask them to circle transitional phrases within paragraphs in red or to underline where they used outside information within their piece. When Renee asked students to look for some similar features in pieces written across the year, they could look for changes aligned with the teaching that transpired within particular studies. What happens after students mark their papers varies. Sometimes Renee asks students to study their visual analysis of a given piece and write their next piece taking into consideration what they did well and attending to missing features or elements that require more of their attention. This doesn't necessarily mean writing another draft of the same piece. When working on essay writing, for example, Renee often asks the kids to write two essays back-to-back so that they can immediately use data from their first attempt to craft a stronger second essay. They then use the same coding scheme to analyze their second essay.

Figure 5.11: Writer's log: Showing the thinking behind the decisions.

Writing work I did today	Why I decided to do this work

After some analysis, writers turn to mapping software to frame their analyses in terms of overall strengths and needs. Using the mapping feature in Inspiration, students begin to articulate what they are seeing in their own writing. For example, as Anders read his essay about different area schools, he cited a strength in his overall writing as, "I had great ending sentences in each paragraph such as the third [paragraph] where I said, 'There are computer classes and any kind of language and things like biology' for the topic, 'there are many opportunities.'" Anders wrote this inside a bubble that he linked to a "Strengths" bubble in his map. Once he had multiple bubbles in his map, he used the Outline View feature to convert his visual analysis into a more traditional outline form. His writing, along with a printed copy of his analysis, became part of his portfolio, which he and his teacher regularly revisited in order to see how his writing habits were changing. Over time, Renee and her students can look at how strengths change, how previous needs become strengths, and what instruction is needed next to help move each writer forward.

At times Anders and his classmates are also called to analyze one another's work. First, they read their peers' work using the coding practices that help them physically identify particular features or ways of thinking. Then, using Renee's guiding questions, they write short paragraphs that summarize what they see in their peers' work. Analyses are shared with writers. Some benefits of this practice are obvious, such as being able to see how others communicate their thinking and connecting specific examples to writing concepts, but, less obviously, it also gives writers another reason to reread and perhaps revise, as was the case with Anders. He explained, "After reading my response again, I think I may have been able to say my thesis in more detail, but it still works the way it is."

Using Feedback for Growth

It's not enough just to"get" feedback. Margin notes such as "awkward" or "nice lead" give writers little to go on if they want to improve their work or figure out how to re-create "nice leads" in future work. All writers need feedback that informs next steps. Oral or written comments can come from peers, teachers, or other readers, but all feedback needs to be relevant, specific, nonthreatening, and timely.

Consider Trevor, an aspiring sixth-grade writer who enjoys writing action-packed narratives about Tobi, an imaginative neighborhood kid who finds himself in precarious situations as he tries to combat his frequent boredom. During a regular weekly visit to Trevor's school, I found him in the office looking for me after his teacher mentioned she'd seen me walk into school earlier that morning. Trevor was anxious to share his now ten-page draft. When I had last seen Trevor, he had written a three-page draft that contained lots of lively scenes but lacked a sense of movement. At that time, we talked about his plans for moving Tobi and his adventures through time. We talked about where the current scenes might lead Tobi, what difficulties he might encounter, and what a character like Tobi might do in response. Reading the ten-page version of the story with Trevor at my side, I listened with delight as he explained what he saw as the main "scenes" in his piece—picking up on language we'd used in our previous discussion. He spoke about how Tobi was soon to discover that the life he was leading was a mirror image of the life his cousin, Ogie, had lived. While the arc of the story was still somewhat in the works, where the scenes were headed was very much on Trevor's mind. But when he talked through the scenes with me, the ten pages seemed very much like a one-paragraph narration. Pulling a chapter book from the classroom library, we began looking at chapter titles and how they named what was to transpire in a particular chapter. We also looked at how dialogue, one of Trevor's favorite writing techniques, was formatted.

Each of the conversations I had with Trevor was an opportunity to collaboratively assess what he was doing well and what advice he needed in order to take the next step. Rather than saying, "good job" or "keep going," I left Trevor with specific feedback anchored in collaborative analysis of his current work. While this piece is still a work in progress, so too is Trevor as a writer. Most recent conversations reveal that he's now working on an autobiography because his writing to date about Tobi had helped him realize that Tobi was very much like him.

From Assessment to Evaluation: The Grades Dilemma

If our vision for writers includes all of the work writers engage with—and an exploration of how writers attend to the world around them, why writers write, how writers can go about their work, and students' personal knowledge of their own actions and decisions as writers is only a part of this work—then reading student writing and assigning a letter grade to the work seems to fall short of meeting our vision. Yet we live in a world that continues to require many of us to boil down the rich writing work alive in our classrooms to a number in an electronic gradebook or a letter grade on a student's report card. One school where I work regularly has moved away from relying solely on letter grade report cards and has spent significant time in the past few years reworking their report cards to include more specific information about student learning. But for most teachers, the choice between assigning single letters or numbers continues to exemplify the systems in which we teach. What can teachers do in situations like this? We might decide to collaborate with our school communities to rework how we summarize and report on learning. We might work with our grade-level colleagues to articulate a rubric of sorts that captures the degrees of progress writers have made during a particular grading period. We might follow Linda Christensen's (2009) lead and outline our expectations for writers in a class syllabus and devise a "total points" scale whereby all kids can earn all points through opportunities for continued revision and learning. The options are many, but here I detail several possibilities drawn from life in public schools.

If becoming a writer involves being familiar with sets of malleable practices, engaging with and refining processes that work best for that writer, and producing pieces that meet intended purposes, then our summative forms of assessment should capture these dimensions. A team of teachers I know came together to discuss the grading dilemma and how they could hang on to their beliefs about the complexities of writing and still be able to enter a grade that reflected shared ways of thinking about the multiple dimensions of writing.

Before you read about how these teachers gathered and used data, let me detail how they thought about the different dimensions of becoming a writer. To ensure that instruction and assessment moved beyond the words printed on page or screen, these teachers used two categories to talk about, think about, and frame the writing in their classrooms: *writing practices* and *written products*. *Practices* referred to the dimensions of the writing curriculum that attend to the behaviors, actions, and processes writers engage in as they progress toward publishing pieces and being successful writers in school and beyond. For the youngest writers, practices might include "writing the best they can," and for more experienced writers these might be "knowing when and where more work on a piece is needed." This dimension also included how writers develop and select ideas, and how writers go about drafting, revising, editing, and eventually publishing their work. Ultimately, this category aimed to capture the different ways in which writers might go about their work so that they can figure out and use what works best for them as they move toward publication. This category also reminded teachers of the importance of exposing kids to many ways of generating ideas, planning, revising, and keeping track of their approaches so that they can work on their writing over time. In contrast, the *written products* dimension focused on what writers created, including the actual words on the pages of drafts and published products.

With these dimensions of writing in mind, we can better understand how this group of teachers envisioned what it meant to become a writer. While they used these dimensions to help frame their regular instructional and assessment practices, they also used these categories to determine grades.

When it came to assessing writers and determining grades, the teachers first decided that they needed ways to attend to writers' practices by using checklists and note taking, strategies discussed earlier in this chapter. Second, they realized that they needed ways of looking at writers' products, the pieces of writing that illustrated the teaching and learning that had transpired within a particular grading period. During the first quarter, for example, instruction had focused a lot on:

- Routines for starting and organizing writing work or time (practices)
- Strategies for sticking with writing and using time well (practices)
- Ways to use published nonfiction to inspire and shape writing (practices)
- Ways to publish students' pieces of nonfiction, specifically looking at ways writers could:
  - organize information in nonfiction text (practices and products)
  - use features of nonfiction such as figures and labels (products)
  - use environmental print for spelling well (practices and products)

These teachers realized that their assessment data needed to align with their teaching focus as well as their vision. In other words, they needed data that would speak to how kids used their time, how well they did sticking with work over time, and how published work influenced students' own pieces. Then these teachers needed to decide on the weight each category would carry for this unit, imagining that these categories would take on different weight over time. While precise percentages might imply averaging, the weights they decided on were really distributions. What they decided was this: At the beginning of the year, most of the summative mark would be based on practices—in this case, the writer's ability to engage in productive routines and stick with the work. The thinking here was that kids first need to be skilled in understanding their responsibilities so that they can get the most out of the year's work. Practices continued to be important but became less of a teaching focus across the year and therefore counted for a smaller weight in the summative grade. Essentially, as kids began to take more responsibility for knowing and enacting their own practices, the pieces they produced became a larger share of a summative mark (see Figure 5.12).

After thinking about the information they wanted to gather and how they might use this information, these teachers then needed to reach consensus about what constituted quality grade 4, grade 6, or whatever grade work with regard to writing practices and products during any given quarter for kids at their school.

5.12: Navigating grading: Valuing practices and products.

	Practices	Products
Quarter I	75%	25%
Quarter II	65%	35%
Quarter III	60%	40%
Quarter IV	50%	50%

Much like the conversations about the on-demand writing pieces discussed at the beginning of this chapter, the conversations did not yield fine-grained rubrics by level but, instead, produced broad and shared understandings of practices that for this school would align with A work, B work, and so on.

During actual grading periods, these teachers had to watch the amount of time they spent on this dimension of summative assessment. It takes time to gain consensus, and teachers had to make room in their schedules for other valued means of communicating who writers were becoming, such as writing narrative comments to connect with formal grades and hosting conversations with parents and guardians about what it means to write well and thus what grades mean in their school context. Nevertheless, while there are many ways to tackle the grading issue, this may be one option you can modify to meet the needs of your particular teaching context.

Another option is to do as Renee does and engage kids in analysis of their work and assign points for engaging in the process. But whatever we decide, we need to consciously think about the forms of assessment that will best benefit young people and contribute to the best teaching and development of lifelong writing skills. And because we'll never be granted more time in our days or more days in our weeks, we need to make decisions about how to use our time in ways that match our visions.

Developing assessment tools and practices that provide meaningful information is key: useful information can lead to informed and intentional teaching and learning—by both teachers and students. Useful information allows writers, teachers, and others to see and celebrate growth over time. And genuine assessment information enables us to speak with confidence about what students need and how classrooms, schools, and policies can be shaped to best meet the needs of diverse learners—and, more specifically, the needs of diverse writers.

Chapter Six

Reaching Outward: Thinking Together about Visions and Decisions

If we want young people to use writing as a tool for thinking, communicating, and actively participating in the creation of a world we want to live in, then young writers and their teachers need shared understandings about writing itself and how people learn to write. But teachers in schools aren't the only ones involved in students' experiences of writing and writing instruction. Other school faculty and staff, administrators, families, communities, and lawmakers all have a hand in shaping understandings of what writing is about and for. Given the diversity of experiences folks in all of these various consituencies bring to the table, we would expect a range of visions and understandings about what it means to learn to write well. How we deal with that range of undertandings matters.

People don't always agree—on daily life issues, social issues, or writing pedagogy and practice issues. Current debates surrounding social issues such as how to best fund and organize schools, how to manage health care, or how to jump-start the economy illustrate the wide range of perspectives people bring to the table. More specific issues involving school or classroom policy—such as when and where conventional spelling ought to be required, how testing impacts curriculum, the role of prompts in writing instruction—give rise to multiple, and oftentimes opposing, stances. It might seem easier for you as a teacher to just avoid a difficult conversation or situation rather than deal with conflicting ideas and perspectives. Or it might seem easier to merely oppose ideas or initiatives rather than offer other possible and viable options. Or it might seem easier to argue vehemently for one way of teaching, one program as opposed to another. But I want to suggest that any of these "easy" stances is less than productive. Merely lobbying hard for this as opposed to that rarely leads another person to switch sides. Opposing options without offering other possibilities doesn't get us very far either. And leaving one context in the hope of finding an already-ideal space for teaching and learning, or finding a program that will meet all student and teacher needs and be the panacea for all writing instructional needs, is also unrealisitic. Rather than avoid difficult conversations, rather than try to make tensions disappear, we need to learn to live within life's tensions and engage in genuine dialogue with others to negotiate understandings that take into consideration the best current knowledge available, the nuances of specific contexts, and the best interests of all young people.

Realistically, then, it is not enough to articulate our own vision for writers or to become aware of the decisions we make, why we make them, and how they affect writers and writing practices. We also need to talk and think with others about what and why we do what we do. This includes engaging with stakeholders close to our classrooms as well as those who may be less familar with daily life in elementary schools. This chapter outlines how we can create spaces for dialogue in which we can learn from and with colleagues, families, community members, and leaders as we make visible our curricular thinking and actions. While some of these constituencies may not share our experiences or thinking about writing, writers, and writing instruction in today and tomorrow's world, making our actions and thinking visible to them can be an important step in inviting and initiating genuine dialogue. Engaging in dialogue in order to think with diverse people and communities can lead to collective visions that result in the best possible curricular decisions being made.

While there are many ways we might connect with people beyond our classrooms, this chapter features activities in the contexts in which I work and learn. I begin close to classrooms and daily school life and then reach out to districts, communities, and other policymakers.

Creating Spaces for Dialogue

Before diving into examples of possible responses and actions we might take to help navigate diverse perspectives, it is important to know that the activities

Creating Spaces for Dialogue

- Collegial collaborations

- Family and community
  collaborations

featured in this chapter are anchored in a fundamental belief about learning and those we learn with—namely, that participants in any learning community become invested members only through legitimate participation (Wenger, 1999). This means that their contributions are real, their activity meaningful, and their understandings defined and refined over time. If we want colleagues, families, policymakers, and others to be invested in what is best for children, we need to engage with them. Engaging *with* means talking, listening, learning, sharing, and rethinking. It means engaging in genuine dialogue.

For some, dialogue might be considered a synonym for talking, which can mean merely presenting information or offering explanations. However, my use here of the word *dialogue* references something deeper and undoubtedly more difficult. Freire and Macedo (1995) write about the necessity of dialogue in all learning, for young and old alike. Dialogue is necessary because knowing and coming to know are social, not individual, processes whereby exploring other people's thoughts, experiences, and actions is central to learning. Therefore, dialogue is about listening and reflecting, learning and growing, not just conveying ideas, defending one's stance, or solving a stated problem. Dialogue is a process through which people grow and change, through which differences are welcomed and needed, through which some problems may be resolved and others arise, and through which people come together to think about issues and ideas. The actions highlighted here aim to move beyond one-way communicative venues to more dialogic activity in which people genuinely talk about what matters most to them, how their experiences shape their thinking, how visions shape their actions, and what actions might best support learners and learning.

As I stated earlier, there are many possible ways in which we could reach out to and think with wider communities. Ultimately, this includes reaching out to and engaging in dialogues with families, community members, and political leaders, audiences I address later in the chapter. This first section features possible ways to reach out to colleagues, highlighting potential venues and actions for collaborative conversations and study about writing, writers, and writing instruction.

Collegial Collaborations

All too often, kids are the only real common denominator in the writing instruction between classrooms. One year they're asked to avoid "worn-out words" as they write stories; another year they're asked to write three conventional sentences each day in their journals in response to a prompt written on the board; another year they're encouraged to use poetic license and write poetry as a vehicle for expression; and in the next year, their study of poetry restricts poetry writing to acrostics, haiku, and cinquains. In the first case, word choice matters; in the second, convention and length trump all other considerations; in the third, decisions and communication are foregrounded; and in the last, following directions prevails. With time, young people generally figure out the rules and norms that shape each classroom space. Some comply; some do not. Some engage with passion and commitment; some do not. Discontinuities make things more difficult for kids as they take on the responsibility for learning and relearning what matters most within a given space and time. Although kids are certainly capable of negotiating this changing terrain, we are capable of doing better to present a unified vision of good writing instruction.

We need to come together with our colleagues so that we share big ideas about writing—including *what* we teach and *how*. This doesn't mean merely divvying up genres across grade levels or mandating pedagogical practices but, rather, coming to consensus about what will guide our writing instruction and rest at the heart of our teaching. It might mean beginning with collective study and then crafting a shared mission or vision statement for writers within a school or even a district. Such a vision could be synthesized from professional readings as well as personal and professional experiences of the writers and writing teachers within a particular community. For example, big ideas could be drawn from *NCTE Beliefs about the Teaching of Writing* or from ideas captured in the NCTE–IRA *Standards for the English Language Arts*, like these:

4. Students adjust their use of spoken, written, and visual language (e.g., conventions, style, vocabulary) to communicate effectively with a variety of audiences and for different purposes.

5. Students employ a wide range of strategies as they write and use different writing process elements appropriately to communicate with different audiences for a variety of purposes.

6. Students apply knowledge of language structure, language conventions (e.g., spelling and punctuation), media techniques, figurative language, and genre to create, critique, and discuss print and nonprint texts.

7. Students conduct research on issues and interests by generating ideas and questions, and by posing problems. They gather, evaluate, and synthesize data from a variety of sources (e.g., print and nonprint texts, artifacts, people) to communicate their discoveries in ways that suit their purpose and audience.

10. Students whose first language is not English make use of their first language to develop competency in the English language arts and to develop understanding of content across the curriculum. (NCTE–IRA, 1996, p. 3)

Whatever the source documents, such ideas could be useful for initiating rich conversations about *what* each statement might mean—in theory and practice. These ideas might facilitate the articulation of unifying statements that capture shared ideas and ideals. A printed mission or vision statement, however, is only as good as the collective actions that bring such language to life. Bringing such language to life requires commitment and collaboration.

Those who spend their days in schools are familiar with the call to collaborate. Organizational structures such as teams suggest collective efforts and strategies to meet common goals. Collaboration is often seen as a must and, in and of itself, is directly linked with success. But in real life, collaborating is often difficult because it requires more than talk—it calls for genuine dialogue. Working and learning together means recognizing strengths in others, taking risks, and making visible what we know, as well as admitting our own learning needs. It means a willingness to try something new, an understanding that mistakes are integral to learning, and a commitment to critical reflection on how collective school practices are meeting students' needs. In many ways, collegial collaborations call for many of the same commitments and conditions that young writers in our classrooms need.

Consider Hadley and Beatrice's story of dialogue, collaboration, and new possibilities. While I've known Hadley for a long time as she's taught at different grade levels within her school, I had the more recent pleasure of meeting her colleague Beatrice and learning how these two teachers began to work together. As Hadley studied critical literacies and writing pedagogy, she continually worked to refine her thinking and practices, yearning for someone to learn with. Upon moving to a first-grade classroom, her opportunities for dialogue seemed to shift. Beatrice, an experienced first-grade teacher, watched Hadley and reflected on her own practices, eventually asking Hadley why she did what she did; Hadley responded in kind, and their conversations continued. Hadley suggested readings, and Beatrice shared her experiences working with a prescribed curriculum. Over time they both made shifts in their practices and shared thinking as they passed each other in the hallway. Then Hadley invited Beatrice to join her in presenting their learning at an upcoming literacy conference. This formal invitation pushed them to devote more intentional time to sitting down to talk, share, listen, and learn from each other. Their work together reached beyond exchanging ideas to inquiring into each other's current beliefs, practices, and visions. While Beatrice and Hadley now strive to create workshop-like environments in which young writers dialogue with published authors, to keep "mental files" (Miller, 2002) of strategies that work for them, and to use technologies to enhance and extend their thinking, the two haven't arrived at a "final answer" regarding what's best for their students. But together they continue to construct new, collective visions and to problem-solve their way to enacting their thinking in their everyday teaching decisions.

Bringing people together to learn from and with one another requires time and explicit effort. Although grade-level teachers are often accustomed to regular meetings, discourse within meetings may be more likely to focus on specific child-study issues or the planning of upcoming field trips or assemblies. Setting aside time for "big ideas" talk is one way to move into deeper dialogue and thinking. In Hadley and Beatrice's case, this came about through the efforts of teacher colleagues, but other school efforts to organize for shared time can move beyond a to-do list to deep thinking about issues of import.

One way to achieve this is through curricular conversations (Mills, Jennings, Donnelley, & Mueller, 2001; Mills, O'Keefe, & Jennings, 2004). Curricular conversations might begin with ten minutes of reading a brief article *during* a meeting, followed by discussion. If professional reading is not a regular practice shared by all, reading during a meeting can work to build such a practice and ensure that all members are familiar with the ideas to be discussed.

A Possible Action: Curricular Conversations

Consider this scenario. An intermediate team takes time to read an excerpt from *Teaching for Joy and Justice* (Christensen, 2009) about building community through poetry and then begins reacting to their reading. As discussion unfolds, it becomes evident that teachers share a common belief in the power of poetry but that their experiences with writing poety—and thus teaching young people to write poetry—vary. While these differences could be perceived as a problem, they could also be seen as an opportunity. Through dialogue this team discovers something they needed to learn. Clarity about what we need to learn is a helpful and necessary first step to helping young people grow as writers. Taking up this opportunity, the team might decide to focus future curricular conversations around teaching and writing poetry. They could select excerpts of professional books to read (such as Georgia Heard's *Awakening the Heart* [1999]), share parts of books written by poets about poetry (such as Ralph Fletcher's *Poetry Matters: Writing a Poem from the Inside Out* [2002]), read interviews with poets (such as the interview with Nikki Giovanni at http://www2.scholastic.com/browse/collateral.jsp?id=10575_type=Contributor_typeId=2604), listen to words of advice from a poet (such as Naomi Shihab Nye's comments on the poetic brillance that children possess at http://www.pbs.org/wgbh/poetryeverywhere/nye.html), view some of Bill Moyer's work (such as the episode "In Praise of Poetry" in his online journal; see http://www.pbs.org/moyers/journal/04252008/profile3.html), or select articles to include in a poetry packet for the team to read and discuss over time. Using a curricular conversation format, the group could convene, share a reading or viewing/listening experience, dialogue, and perhaps write (a poem or two might be appropriate here).

Collective conversation can lead to greater insight into one another's thoughts and reasoning, whether about poetry or another issue. If a team struggles to define a specific issue, regularly turning to a particular publication could be another approach to initiating curricular conversations. For example, recent issues of *School Talk* contain brief articles about young children reading and writing in a digital world (Garcia & Chiki, 2010a, 2010b), writing in the content areas (Johnson & Chiki, 2009b), and supporting our youngest writers (Johnson & Chiki, 2009a). Articles such as these as well as popular media articles are brief and offer a perspective from which to elicit individuals' thinking and experiences. Over time, team members can come to see, recognize, and use one another's strengths as they work together across their classrooms with kids' best interests at heart.

A Possible Action: Study Groups

When reading short pieces in face-to-face contexts or engaging in experience-based dialogues falls short of meeting learning goals, teachers can also develop shared-interest study groups. As a member of a multiyear elementary study group focused on writing with members from three schools within the same district, I was able to participate as we selected professional literature to read outside our discussion time. Over the years, we read books such as *A Fresh Look at Writing* (Graves, 1994) and *Wondrous Words* (Ray, 1999). We decided on what and how much to read before our meetings and then met monthly after school to share classroom actions that grew from our readings—making visible our successes as well as those experiences that didn't go as planned. We also accepted invitations from Georgia Heard (1995) and Natalie Goldberg (2010) that engaged us in our own personal writing and sharing. Sharing our processes, practices, struggles, and concerns as writers opened spaces for dialogue that moved us beyond idea sharing to intent listening, learning, and growing as a community of learners, writers, and teachers.

A Possible Action: Vertical Team Meetings

Although dialogues among adults with shared interests or similar jobs (e.g., grade-level positions) are important, so too are efforts to reach across the multiple years of students' learning lives. If our concern is about who young people become as writers, thinkers, decision makers, and citizens, we need to think and work intentionally so that our focus is on students' lifelong and life-wide learning. One way we might respond to this challenge is by reaching out to neighboring grade-level colleagues. To create a space for dialogue among teachers across grade levels, one school incorporates vertical team meetings into their monthly meeting rotation. One week they meet as grade-level teams, another week in vertical teams (such as preK–2, 3–5, 6–8), another week with specialists, and so forth. Faculty meetings focus on covering "school business" so that team talk can focus on curricular issues. Teams set their own agendas and take minutes in their team binder, and school leaders rotate where and when they participate in these dialogues. Early in the year, for example, primary teachers discussed possibilities for curriculum night—how could they move it beyond "showing completed kid work" to engaging families in school experiences? Together they brainstormed activities ranging from science demonstrations, to child-led math games, to websites and technology stations. They also discussed communication practices with families and how different classrooms were reaching out to families, including forums and languages used. Together they decided to create a primary curriculum night information sheet in multiple languages, with various team members lending their linguistic expertise to assist monolingual teachers. Although dialogues such as these are central to adult learning, they certainly affect student learning.

These actions constitute a few ways to help create a collaborative spirit with colleagues. While this kind of reaching outward is vital to our success as teachers and to the success of the kids we teach, it is not the only outreach we need to make. In the next section, I offer some possibilities for why and how we must extend the notion of dialogue to include the families of those we teach.

Family and Community Collaborations

If we are to work collaboratively with the best interests and intentions regarding who children become as writers and more, we need to work in partnership with families. Partnerships are anchored in trusting, caring relationships, which means families must be and feel welcome in schools. JoBeth Allen (2007) wrote a wonderful book about this topic, *Creating Welcoming Schools*, in which she emphasizes the importance of valuing the resources and assets that kids bring with them to school, and details how every move made by the adults in a school—from office clerks to coaches, custodians, security guards, faculty, and administration—matters in creating productive and welcoming learning spaces. She highlights a community photography project as one that school communities might take up as they work to create supportive learning environments. Another option might be to schedule regular times or events that bring families together within the school in simple yet important ways.

A Possible Action: Library Nights

Consider library nights. One public school I work with launched these events with their school community, dedicating regular nights to welcoming students and their families into the library for reading, collective book checkout, and simple book making. The preparations are minimal, the impact significant. On the first library night of the year, the library was packed. Students read to family members, and family members worked with students. With no formal program, no set conference or meeting, this space simply invited family and school members to read, talk, and learn together. Parents, grandparents, siblings, and guardians read picture books with young children and one another; students sought the principal's advice on finding a good book; one young reader found a recent in-class read-aloud, a Magic Tree House book in Spanish, and began reading her favorite parts aloud to her accompanying family member; a girl and her mother pored over a Chicago architecture book, talking about the buildings they'd seen, not yet seen, and planned to find; another young reader and I explored the world of Babymouse (Holm & Holm, 2005) and the ways in which words and images are integrated to tell the story. This informal yet important venue not only provides families with a window into life in school, but it also gives other members of the school community insight into the relationships, practices, interests, and resources of students and their caregivers.

A Possible Action: Weekly Workshops

Another public school offered regular weekly workshops (Vopat, 1994) focused on experiential learning opportunities for adult family members. Some workshops engaged adults with their children in shared projects, as when families worked with second-grade readers and writers to write their own family memories along the lines of Carmen Lomas Garza's (Garza, Rohmer, & Alarcón, 2000) picture book *In My Family/En Mi Familia*. Working with teachers and their child, families wrote bilingual texts and published their work, which is now displayed alongside a permanent mural they painted on the second floor of their school building. Another year, as the school endeavored to facilitate dialogue among members of a changing school community, adult family members gathered while their children were in class to write poetry, read and discuss novels, and use literature to explore their diverse cultural lives (see Figure 6.1) (Van Sluys, Cambron, Perez, Garcia, Rosales, & Ramirez, 2008).

Library nights, workshops, and other opportunities for families to get to know one another and the school form a solid foundation for engaging in dialogue with others and coming to share visions and subsequent decisions for children regarding children's literacy lives.

A Possible Action: Written Correspondence

Technologies and creative professional thinking offer numerous ways to use print to reach out and connect with adults in our students' lives. We can publish newsletters collaboratively authored by students and the teacher, as illustrated in

Figure 6.1: Family perspectives: Learning together.

Chapter 3 by Aimee and her second graders. We might use written conversation in notebooks, class webpages, and blogs as additional spaces for exchanging thinking. While the venues are many, what we write and how we write it is worth considering if we want to move beyond sharing information to inviting dialogue. For example, at the beginning of the year, we can invite caregivers to write us letters or send us emails sharing what they think is important to know about their child as a person, learner, and writer. The invitation may be open-ended or based on guiding questions to encourage families to highlight what they see as their child's assets and needs. This also means that responses may be in languages other than English, which will require enlisting the help of others knowledgeable in languages spoken in students' homes. Taking the time to find people to help translate letters is well worth it, as the insights gained from families is often invaluable, and a beginning-of-the-year invite such as this often sets the tone for collaboration in the year(s) to come.

Beyond the beginning-of-the-year letter, we might follow Stephanie's lead; she creates backpacks with plush animals that "visit" her first graders' homes. As Tomás the Take-Home Tiger and friends rotate among class members' homes, children teach the visitor something and then write about what they taught their stuffed friend. When first graders share their writing during their morning meeting, both teacher and classmates learn many things. For example, after Tomás the Take-Home Tiger spent the night at Omar's, we learned that Tomás was taught to make a birdhouse. We also learned that it was Omar's older brother who helped and that Omar too was learning to construct things under his brother's guidance. We learned that this brother guides Omar in many ways, including his writing work.

While we can extend many different types of invitations and elicit different types of contributions, how we respond and use the information is critical. When we learn about the talents, what Moll has called "funds of knowledge" (2001), that are alive in diverse households, we need to draw on those resources throughout the school day, within and beyond our decisions related to the writing curriculum. When family members offer their assessments of their children as writers, we need to combine their insights with our own to make the best decisions possible.

Inviting and soliciting input from students' beyond-school lives is valuable, but so too is making visible in-school thinking and experiences. Just stating what we believe or giving beginning-of-the-year descriptions of classroom life often isn't enough. We need to share what is happening in school, explain why, and invite response in ongoing ways. For example, we need to demonstrate how we teach grammar in context, show how writers take responsibility for their work, and show how our questioning leads writers to new places without dictating agendas that writers must pursue. We might do this by posting student work-in-progress on our class webpage, include information about the process learners are engaged in, and use the comment feature to invite reader input. Another way to make visible school activity is through the use of "Dear Writer" letters. A "Dear Writer" letter, as defined by one intermediate classroom teacher and writing community, is a beginning-of-the-unit letter that outlines where the class will be heading in the weeks to come. Notice in the bottom half of the letter in Figure 6.2 the assessment tool that, at the beginning, helps students create a vision for where they're going and the practices they will be called on to learn more about and use in their writing work. At the very bottom of the sheet is a space for both family and student signatures, since the teacher wants writers to talk not only with classmates and her about their writing work but also with folks at home. This "Dear Writer" letter is an assessment and evaluation tool to be used within the unit of study, but it also provides a framework and tool for dialogue as students, teachers, and beyond-school supporters progress through a given curriculum unit.

Figure 6.2: "Dear Writer" letter: "Stories That Make Me Who I Am."

Stories that Make Me Who I Am

Dear Writer,

Your first writing project is complete, and you are on your way to writing your second personal narrative. You have amazed me with your growth, but we still have a long way to go. By now you have gathered many "seeds" in your writer's notebook and I am hopeful that you will choose the most significant one to publish.

By the end of this project, writer, you will be able to:

- Successfully engage in the five steps of the writing process (Rehearse, Draft, Revise, Edit, Publish)
- Consider your audience by choosing stories that are meaningful & interesting
- Write with focus and clarity
- Write an organized narrative with a clear beginning, middle & end
- Compose captivating lead and ending paragraphs
- Use figurative language and repetition to enhance your writing
- Write using true exact details
- Paragraph properly
- Write using complete sentences
- Use and punctuate dialogue properly
- Produce sentences with proper subject/verb agreement & proper verb tense

Remember, you are the expert on the topic of your life. When you write stories from your own experience, you already have a plot. Your job will be to make the story interesting - as interesting for your reader as it was for you when it happened. Lots of description, lots of action, and lots of dialogue will help your reader feel what you felt. Below is a rubric that will be used to assess your final work. Use it as a guide in your writing. Good Luck! ♥

Features	Descriptors	Comments
Focus	My story is meaningful & Interesting (Rule of SO WHAT?) I have an interesting start to my personal narrative that catches the reader's attention (LEAD PARAGRAPH) My entire personal narrative is about a **clearly focused** topic/event. I write a **closing/ending** paragraph that effectively unifies my writing. [There is a lesson learned or a realization]	
Support/Elaboration	I use **figurative language and repetition to enhance my writing.** I elaborate using true, exact details (Show don't tell)	
Organization	My personal narrative moves logically through time and has a **beginning, middle, and an ending**. I use **paragraphing** to help organize my narrative.	
Conventions	I use **complete sentences.** I use and **punctuate dialogue** properly. I spell familiar words correctly. I use capitalization and punctuation correctly. I make sure that the **subject of my sentence agrees with the verb.** I use the same **verb tense** throughout my composition.	

Student Signature _____

Parent Signature _____

A Possible Action: Publication Celebrations

At the end of a unit of study, students often publish their work. Rather than simply having students turn in their publications for teacher evaluation, teachers can create rituals that encourage continued learning for both writer and readers. Consider this publication celebration in a primary classroom where kids had written picture books. When family and community members were invited to school for the celebration, young people were asked not only to "share their story" but also to teach others what they knew about writing. Instead of asking each child to read his or her book to a large audience, running the risk that audience members might grow restless and thus limit each student's opportunity to read, student books were displayed around the room with response sheets. For the first fifteen minutes, authors remained with their books and read them to visitors. After listening to a book, visitors provided the author with a written comment. Then both visitors and author moved around the room to read and comment on as many books as they could. In this particular celebration, we noticed a marked difference between adult and young writers' comments. Visitors wrote comments like "I loved your book" and "Great job!" and young writers wrote comments to peers like "I loved how you made the words get bigger just like Donald Crews did," or "I want to know what happened on your next fishing trip." Comments reflected commentors' experiences with responding to texts. Some visitors began to pick up on children's specific comments and offered a few more specific thoughts. While young people liked to hear that readers enjoyed their books, they were especially glad when readers noticed the specific things they had worked hard to accomplish in the writing of their books, such as emulating respected authors and making readers crave sequels.

A Possible Action: Documentation Boards

Another way to provide windows into the visions and decisions alive in classrooms is through the use of documentation boards akin to those displayed in Reggio Emilia schools (Hertzog, 2001), where both processes and pedagogical thinking are made visible. In one school where I work with young writers, their teachers, and preservice teacher candidates, documentation boards fill the school hallways and classrooms. Photographs capture the work of students as they explore science concepts, work with math manipulatives to pose and solve problems, express themselves through art and movement, and use literature and writing to engage with one another and the world. Captions—in both teacher and student words—detail the thinking that accompanies activity. As my preservice teachers and I spent regular time with young writers and their teachers, we too used photos to capture our engagement with this community of learners, documenting the decisions that reflected our, and the school's, vision. In Figure 6.3, you can see a photo of a group of student writers paired with photos of classroom artifacts. These grouped photos

Figure 6.3: Documenting growth: Valuing and explaining writers' development.

 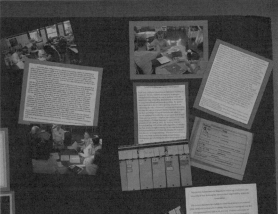

illustrate various stages or ways in which writers developed understandings of print over time as they scribbled, drew, and used alphabetic principles, phonetics, and reading experiences to transcribe their thinking into print. The accompanying typed explanations share not only *what* is contained within the photos, but also *why* the images captured matter in the overall life of children and their learning.

A Possible Action: Professional Conversations

We can also invite families and visitors into our schools, through more structured curriculum meetings, as well as through more open-ended, dialogic experiences, to help them learn about the ways in which writing unfolds. When one school community took a more process and workshop approach to writing instruction, the educators there knew that classroom activity looked different from many of their family and community members' experiences of writing in school. Therefore, the principal and other educators in the school community offered evening meetings to let others discuss and see the instruction and learning of writing in action. Using video footage taken in their school, these educators invited families to watch a mini-lesson, observe students and teachers interact during writing time, and see, hear, and debrief what they saw and wondered about. The initiating agenda for these meetings was to communicate how instruction was unfolding in their classrooms and why, so the ensuing conversation, both lively and insightful, was satisfying for all involved.

A less formal type of meeting, referred to as a coffee talk, is a venue used in another school to discuss family questions and concerns and school decisions. Coffee talks are hosted at various times during the year and day. Often held in the mornings after students begin class, adults, sometimes accompanied by their younger children, gather together with administrators and teacher leaders to discuss issues on their minds. Topics range from questions and concerns about bilingual programs to curriculum and safety. In one instance, a college undergraduate interested in pursuing a career in teaching attended a bilingual coffee talk, learned about adult family members' interest in improving their English, and subsequently began offering adult English classes for interested adults. What participants discuss, learn, and do as a result of coffee talks depends on what is brought to the table and the collective will of the participants to take action on their thinking.

A Possible Action: Getting to Know the Community Scavenger Hunt

It is often the case that teachers work in neighborhoods and cities or towns different from where they live. Who owns the corner restaurant, who works in the community library, where kids go and who they spend their time with after school, and where family members work are often unexplored mysteries. To immerse elementary teachers in their teaching community, one school incorporated a scavenger hunt of sorts into their beginning-of-the-year professional development. Collecting actual objects was not the primary focus of the hunt; teachers worked in teams to visit places in the neighborhood, introduce themselves, and begin to imagine ways to connect and collaborate with community members.

As teachers visited local businesses, a neighboring high school, libraries, city offices, and so forth, their thinking was guided by prompts such as "You're interested in setting up a mentorship relationship for one of your students" and "You're embarking on a gardening project." The prompts and teachers' experiences introducing themselves, talking with community members, and exploring neighboring contexts helped teachers initiate important relationships for collaborative work and meaningful dialogue in the months and years to follow.

A Possible Action: Advocating for Writers in the Wider World

Actions shared thus far have been anchored in the local lives of schools. Because decisions that impact school life are also made in spaces beyond schools, it is essential that we connect with others who live and work in those spaces. Most likely these others are not educators by profession and therefore would benefit from developing a more nuanced understanding of teaching, learning, life in schools, and, more specifically, what it means to become a writer in the twenty-first century and beyond. We can go about this in many different ways, but building relationships and engaging in genuine dialogue are key.

Working with various schools has made it clear to me that politicians and community leaders like to be present for ribbon cuttings and special events. Welcome their presence and participation, and make it a learning experience.

Use documentation boards to illustrate learning processes, ask children to be tour guides and to talk about their learning experiences, and use video to demonstrate learning in action. As relationships grow, involve community leaders in new ways. One school, for example, was working on a community action project regarding their school yard landscape. Students were leading a campaign to convert their asphalt play lot into a space that supported safe play and reflected their school's environmental commitments. Kids wrote and filmed public service announcements (PSAs), which involved conducting an interview with the alderman. A final version of the PSA, complete with bilingual subtitles, was shared at community presentations as well as with the alderman's office. Experiences like this make visible that young people are writing more than essays and that they are using multiple languages to communicate. They also position young people as civic- and socially minded leaders making decisions about how to use their literacies for genuine agendas, and who need community support for time and resources to make these sorts of learning endeavors a norm for all learners.

As educators we also need to reach out to our state and national legislators to establish proactive relationships. Our representatives need people to turn to as they shape their understandings of education—and we need to become those people. Although policymakers may seem distant to us and skepticism about the value of our input may cause us to hesitate, many anecdotal experiences have taught me that it never hurts to try; you might be pleasantly surprised to discover how much your experiences and perspectives do matter. While we might wish that our legislators are experienced literacy educators, they often are not—but we are. We know that writing is complex work; we know that first graders can write powerful poetry, that fourth graders can craft strong written arguments for ideas they genuinely care about, that writers new to English require years of experience to learn to use conversational and academic language conventionally and that their emergent writing ought not to be understood as a complete representation of their thinking; and we know that making time for writing supports young people's development as writers, as readers, as citizens. And we have the expertise to talk about such points, not just in theory but in practice as well, by drawing from everyday lived experiences in classrooms. Our experiences and expertise can teach others that writing is more than proper grammar, neat handwriting, and formulaic essays.

Last year while meeting with legislators in Washington as part of NCTE's Advocacy Day, one teacher who had traveled to DC had the chance to visit her state's senator. In recounting this experience, she explained how she used classroom examples to illustrate for him the need for writing instruction to be part of all young people's school lives, and how the effectiveness of teachers' work with kids was a much more complex endeavor than current discourse might suggest. She was surprised that her senator then handed her actual legislation and asked for her comments. Another teacher who also attended Advocacy Day reflected on how she was beginning to see different possibilities for her role as an advocate. She was somewhat frustrated with the reception she received at the state level, but she seemed to find possibilities for next steps now that she had connected with her representative's Washington office. Perseverance was key, she explained. There's plenty of work to do, but sometimes it requires time and effort to discover where our voice might matter most.

Along with hopeful stories are challenges, uncomfortable moments, and frustration. Consider one teacher's experience upon her return home from Washington just in time for state testing. She shared with her class her positive interactions with legislators who listened when she told them about the needs of new English language learners, the time and experience needed to use English well, and the need to differently assess what kids know and need. But once home, the disparity between these positive interactions and the reality of school hit immediately: she was still required to administer state tests in English. Geraldo, a student who had been in the United States for only a year, quickly became frustrated when no help could be given and began to cry. A classmate turned to the teacher and said, "They [policymakers] need to work faster; Geraldo is crying." While our experience tells us that Geraldo isn't the only one who needs schooling, learning, and assessment to change, this story also emphasizes the importance of this work.

We all need not journey to Washington; we can make our thinking known through appointments with aides and politicians in our local communities, regular emails expressing our positions and sharing relevant resources, and letters sent directly to policymakers or community members via editorial forums. When doing so, we need to know what our "asks" are. This means knowing, in a focused way, what we want to see happen and why our "asks" matter. There are many places you can turn for recent research and resources that can help inform you and ultimately shape conversations: documents like *NCTE Beliefs about the Teaching of Writing*, other policy documents, and NCTE's annual legislative platform. Using these resources and our own experiences as a base, we then need to speak clearly—generally without our professional jargon—to share what we want for learners and why. Also keep in mind that although stories of what's not working are valuable, we need suggestions and possible alternatives for what we might do well in order to help our nation do what is right for kids as writers and citizens. In the words of one teacher, we need to enter into conversations "ready to talk from [our] experiences, ready to listen, and ready to learn" as we come to the table with experiences and perspectives to offer the folks we're talking with.

Genuine dialogue is about exchanging ideas, thinking together, and collaboratively generating possible next steps. Being proactive, being in the conversations, and being a learner can help us to create the best possible policies, conditions, and classrooms for all.

Becoming a Writer

Becoming a writer is about developing voice, taking a stand, and using language to communicate thinking to genuine audiences, including oneself. Becoming a writer calls for supportive communities in which visions and decisions are both shared and evolving.

Becoming a writer means engaging in activity that is both personal and social—activity that is much more complex than implementing someone else's plan. Becoming a writer requires confidence—knowing that your voice matters, that writers often figure out their thinking en route, and that people will respond with respect and support for your efforts.

Becoming a writer in school calls for classroom environments that are designed to help young people understand what we know about the enduring habits and practices writers employ and how they can become open to new possibilities. Becoming a strong teacher of young writers means developing and reflecting on our visions; making and sharing our decisions with students; engaging responsively with student moves, difficulties, and inquiries; taking students' lives, interests, questions, and contributions seriously; and crafting curriculum that focuses on the young people who walk in, and out, of our classroom. Being a strong teacher of young writers means striving to develop strong writers, who write well now and who are prepared to continue to do so into the future.

As we strive to create spaces in which teachers and young people know what they're doing, why they're doing it, and how their work impacts who they are now as well as who they are becoming, we might continually ask ourselves questions like these:

- How are we articulating our understandings about where we've been and where we're going with respect to writing, writers, and writing instruction? And with whom are we articulating this?

- How are student agency and decision making invited and supported within our approach to writing instruction?

- For what reasons are students writing in school? Beyond school?

- What types of texts are students reading, composing, and designing?

- In what ways are classroom structures and practices encouraging collaborative and ongoing reflection about decisions made and the impact or consequences of such decisions?

- What opportunities are present, sought out, or created to engage teachers in continuous learning about writing in today and tomorrow's world?

Questions like these, professional organization resources, colleagues, students, communities, and the changes that characterize the contexts in which we teach and learn can push us to continually reexamine our understandings and actions. There's much work to be done and no single blueprint or set of answers to guarantee success. But if we are to change our world so that young people can understand and use writing in powerful ways, such changes will come from the hard, creative, thoughtful, and caring actions of people—including educators, and including me and you.

As we reach the end of these pages, I invite you to accept one more invitation, an invitation that will encourage you to look ahead to see what you might do next.

Possible Actions: Articulating My Next Steps

Take time to reflect on and review your current vision for writing, writers, and writing instruction in light of your experiences reading this book. Given your vision and the contexts in which you teach, consider possible actions and make a commitment regarding what you will do next to improve the lives and experiences of the young writers in your care.

Right now, this is what I can do to impact the present and future life of writers . . .

Annotated Bibliography

Atwell, Nancie.
Lessons That Change Writers.
Portsmouth, NH: Heinemann, 2007. Print.

Atwell offers readers images of her best mini-lesson experiences from teaching and learning with her middle-grade writers. This book emerged from Atwell's commitment to animating what responsive teaching might look like in action. While the heart of the book features scripted mini-lessons that focus on topics, principles, genres, and conventions, Atwell herself notes her hesitations and thoughts about offering scripted lessons. She emphasizes that lessons are scaffolds intended for teachers to try on, modify, and adapt to meet the needs of writers in their classrooms. They are lessons her students have deemed useful and important, and they are images of what might or could be, not what must be. The lessons urge teachers to make wise curricular decisions that move students beyond school genres and conventions to writing well in ways that the world genuinely demands.

Bomer, Katherine.
Hidden Gems: Naming and Teaching from the Brilliance in Every Student's Writing.
Portsmouth, NH: Heinemann, 2010. Print.

The words contained within the covers of this book are not only eloquent but also necessary for every teacher who works to nurture strong, confident writers who can reach their readers. Bomer contends that teachers need experience noticing and naming what kids can do in their writing. She offers readers ways to learn to see and talk about the brilliant, and often intentional, moves writers make so that teachers can communicate to kids what they've achieved and where they might head next. Bomer urges teachers to find ways of assessing and responding that *teach* rather than sort, fail to challenge, or humiliate students. This book stretches teachers of writers by offering strategies for responding to writing, suggesting practices for reading and learning from student writing alone and with colleagues, and calling for the repositioning of dominant definitions of assessment so that assessment affirms who students are while stretching them to new places.

Christensen, Linda.
Teaching for Joy and Justice: Re-imagining the Language Arts Classroom.
Milwaukee: Rethinking Schools, 2009. Print.

Christensen offers readers images and strategies of classroom practices that urge questioning, action, change, and justice. Drawing from her life as a secondary language arts educator and from critical pedagogy, she explores topics such as poetry, essay, and narrative writing; language and power; and response to student work. Throughout, she emphasizes the power of meaningful content, the roles of students' lives and languages in their learning, and the charge for educators to teach, not assign, writing. While readers can easily borrow the curricular options she offers for immediate use in their own classrooms, Christensen's detailed reasoning regarding the value she places on any given activity urges readers instead to think about when, why, and how they might explore such issues and to borrow ideas from her work. And, while the activities featured reflect life in secondary classrooms, Christensen's wise thinking, powerful examples, rich resources, and deep rationales make this a resource for all teachers committed to creating a just world through engaging, relevant, and joyful learning experiences in schools.

Corgill, Ann Marie.
Of Primary Importance: What's Essential in Teaching Young Writers.
Portland, ME: Stenhouse, 2008. Print.

Corgill wrote the professional book she most wanted to read. She notes that her book isn't a step-by-step guide, but rather a window into the lively writing lives in her primary classrooms. Her opening chapter defines the "essentials" of asking, analyzing, applauding, assisting, assessing, and advocating as teachers work to create the best possible writing curricula for their students. Subsequent chapters explore how teachers might go about creating the spaces in which curriculum can come to life. Specifically, she attends to studies of poetry, nonfiction writing, and picture books, as well as publication and ways to move all writers forward. Through classroom vignettes, examples of student writing, and reflections, Corgill asks readers to consider what her experiences and decisions might mean for other classroom teachers interested in teaching young writers well.

Freeman, David, and Yvonne Freeman.
Essential Linguistics: What You Need to Know to Teach Reading, ESL, Spelling, Phonics, and Grammar.
Portsmouth, NH: Heinemann, 2004. Print.

While the subtitle suggests that this book is a tool for exploring issues related to reading pedagogy, it primarily offers insight into language itself and how it is learned. The Freemans argue that the more teachers know about how language works, the more they will understand the processes that take place, the approximations and decisions made, as kids develop as language users—as writers, readers, and talkers. As the authors walk readers through theories of language learning, such as phonology, orthography, and morphology, they do so in a way that is clear, accessible, and directly applicable to classroom practice. With deep understandings of language and language learning, teachers can make wise decisions for all learners—both those for whom English is their

first language and those who are adding English to their linguistic repertoire.

Fu, Danling.
Writing between Languages: How English Language Learners Make the Transition to Fluency, Grades 4–12.
Portsmouth, NH: Heinemann, 2009. Print.

Fu focuses on older learners, detailing the ways in which learners who are new to English can make the best use of their literacy knowledge in their first language as they add English to their literacy repertoire. Fu uses student work examples to explore and illustrate important concepts, including second language writing development, code-switching, interlanguage, and more, as a way to help teachers working with writers new to English. She challenges educators to move beyond response to mere surface features of writing to become readers who see and respond to students' thinking.

Graves, Donald H.
A Fresh Look at Writing.
Portsmouth, NH: Heinemann, 1994. Print.

This book has been a longtime favorite of mine, as Graves was among the first authors I knew who wrote about writing with young people. The book takes an action-oriented approach to writing instruction in which you're asked to engage in short exercises as you read. Particularly appropriate for study groups, the book can help you add another layer of thinking about how to approach writers and writing instruction. While Graves invites active thinking and doing, he also shares his experiences, wisdom, and ideas about how we help children begin and continue writing. He outlines conditions for effective writing, makes suggestions about classroom organization and routines, and responds to issues often on teachers' minds, such as assessment, conventions, spelling, and working with families. He also dedicates a section of the book specifically to curriculum and explores how to engage in the study and writing of fiction, nonfiction, and poetry. This book is a staple in a teacher's professional library.

Johnston, Peter H.
Choice Words: How Our Language Affects Children's Learning.
Portland, ME: Stenhouse, 2004. Print.

While this book may not have *writing* in the title nor contain lesson ideas focused exclusively on writing instruction, I consider it an essential text for all educators. Whether teaching, conferring, or providing feedback, we are using language to communicate. In doing so, we are not just stating our opinion or sharing our knowledge and experience about particular content; we are forging relationships with learners and, with our every move, contributing to how students see themselves, the world, and their place in it. Peter Johnston skillfully invites readers to explore how language use (written or spoken) impacts learning. Teachers I know who have read this book walk away thinking about their role and the possible impact their actions can have in the learning lives of young people in their classrooms and schools.

Lewison, Mitzi, Christine Leland, and Jerome C. Harste.
Creating Critical Classrooms: K–8 Reading and Writing with an Edge.
Mahwah, NJ: Lawrence Erlbaum Associates, 2007. Print.

Writers craft their words to accomplish particular, social work. What is said, how it is said, as well as what is unsaid all matter. If we want young people to use their language skills to work in and on the world, then we need to pay close attention to what we include (and perhaps exclude) from our classroom curriculum. This book explores reading and writing practices in real classroom settings and examines how a critical approach to literacy might unfold in diverse spaces. The authors not only explore key concepts, such as cultural resources, language study, and social action, but also look at how children's literature and lived experiences can help kids become critical consumers and users of language. The book features numerous invitations that can be used in classrooms to engage readers and writers in important thinking and actions.

Newkirk, Thomas, and Lisa C. Miller, eds.
The Essential Don Murray: Lessons from America's Greatest Writing Teacher.
Portsmouth, NH: Heinemann, 2009. Print.

As teachers of writers, we must not only be writers ourselves but also learn from the skilled writing teachers who have made it their life's work to demystify writing. Compiled as a tribute to writing teacher extraordinaire Don Murray, this collection of Murray's work offers readers a taste of his wise words and constantly evolving thinking. Essays feature Murray thinking about writing as a recursive, evolving process of rehearsing, drafting, and revising. They also connect theories with practice in a way that moves beyond easily "teachable parts" to genuine learning experiences. Snippets from Murray's daybook offer readers a glimpse of the tools and practices this man used to write and study his own activity and thinking. Other pieces trace the processes and thinking that emerged at specific times in his writing life. Taken as a whole, this collection illustrates enduring aspects of the art and craft of writing well.

Ray, Katie Wood.
What You Know by Heart: How to Develop Curriculum for Your Writing Workshop.
Portsmouth, NH: Heinemann, 2002. Print.

Katie Wood Ray invites readers to learn from their own lives as readers and writers. Too often, she suggests, we jump right into teacher mode without taking the time to live reflectively as readers and writers, to figure out what is really happening to us as we read and write, and to consider what that means for writing instruction. This book invites and guides readers to do just that. Ray notes that this is not a comprehensive book about entire writing programs, but rather is concerned with the heart of good writing instruction—good curriculum and a well-informed teacher. Using a two-column structure, Ray walks us through the curricular chunks and thinking behind moves made in our own writing lives, the writing lives of published authors, and mini-lessons that grow from our experiences. Readers will walk away with a comprehensive understanding of how to form genuine curricular statements that reflect the real work of writing well, in addition to strategies and resources useful for teaching these ideas well.

Ray, Katie Wood, and Lester L. Laminack.
The Writing Workshop: Working through the Hard Parts (and They're All Hard Parts).
Urbana, IL: NCTE, 2001. Print.

While there are many resources on the topic, this book is one I find myself recommending again and again as I work with folks who raise the question of what exactly is meant by *writing workshop*. Rather than defining writing workshop as one particular thing, Ray and Laminack dissect and explore key issues for teachers to consider as they bring to life writing workshop in their own school contexts. The book works from the premise that creating a writing workshop is hard work and involves more than implementing particular units or lessons; rather, good teaching needs to be embedded in a context in which the tone is right, in which writers are granted predictable times and rituals, in which learners not only believe that they are writers but also are surrounded with teaching that supports their development, in which assessment is ongoing and used to inform instruction, and in which lessons and units are well planned and sequenced to meet writers' needs. Individual chapters, while not prescriptive, are clear and comprehensive. Not only do I

consistently recommend this book, but I also consistently receive feedback from teacher colleagues that this was just the right resource to help them structure the kind of writing workshop in their schools and classrooms that suits their students.

Routman, Regie.
Writing Essentials: Raising Expectations and Results While Simplifying Teaching.
Portsmouth, NH: Heinemann, 2005. Print.

Routman, like Atwell, invites readers to think about writing instruction in simple, essential ways. "Simplifying" teaching does not mean making it easier but rather focusing on what is most important by consolidating teacher knowledge of writing, what writers do, and the strengths and needs of specific students. Routman defines what is truly essential for writers to understand—from sense of audience, the role of relevant topics, and the options for organization to the power of language and the need for reading, rereading, revision, and conventions—and how teaching can support these essentials. After making the case for a simplified set of essentials (versus the search for a "perfect program" that doesn't exist), the remaining four sections explore these essentials in more detail: the organization, structure, and practices possible within writing classrooms; the importance of advocacy; and the basics of lesson planning. The book also includes a CD with sample student writing and short videos of conferences. This resource provides a foundation for educators interested in creating classroom curriculum and structures that are anchored in informed beliefs and understandings about the true work of writers.

Works Cited

Allen, J. (2007). *Creating welcoming schools: A practical guide to home–school partnerships with diverse families.* New York: Teachers College Press.

Anderson, C. (2000). *How's it going? A practical guide to conferring with student writers.* Portsmouth, NH: Heinemann.

Anderson, C. (2005). *Assessing writers.* Portsmouth, NH: Heinemann.

Anderson, D. D. (2008). The elementary persuasive letter: Two cases of situated competence, strategy, and agency. *Research in the Teaching of English, 42*(3), 270–314.

Applegate, K. (2007). *Home of the brave.* New York: Square Fish.

Atwell, N. (1987). *In the middle: Writing, reading, and learning with adolescents.* Portsmouth, NH: Boynton/Cook.

Atwell, N. (1998). *In the middle: New understandings about writing, reading, and learning.* Portsmouth, NH: Boynton/Cook.

Barbieri, M. (2002). *Change my life forever: Giving voice to English language learners.* Portsmouth, NH: Heinemann.

Barton, D., Hamilton, M., & Ivanič, R. (1999). *Situated literacies: Reading and writing in context.* New York: Routledge.

Bomer, R. (1995). *Time for meaning: Crafting literate lives in middle and high school.* Portsmouth, NH: Heinemann.

Bomer, R., & Bomer, K. (2001). *For a better world: Reading and writing for social action.* Portsmouth, NH: Heinemann.

Bomer, R., Zoch, M. P., David, A. D., & Ok, H. (2010). New literacies in the material world. *Language Arts, 88*(1), 9–20.

Boscolo, P. (2008). Writing in primary school. In C. Bazerman (Ed.), *Handbook of research on writing: History, society, school, individual, text.* New York: Routledge.

Brown, M. (2007). *Butterflies on Carmen Street.* Houston: Piñata Books.

Cazden, C., Cope, B., Fairclough, N., Gee, J., Kalantzis, M., Kress, G., Luke, A., Luke, C., Michaels, S., & Nakata, M. (1996). A pedagogy of multiple literacies: Designing social futures. *Harvard Educational Review, 66*(1), 60–92.

Calkins, L. (1986). *The art of teaching writing.* Portsmouth, NH: Heinemann.

Calkins, L. (1994). *The art of teaching writing.* Portsmouth, NH: Heinemann.

Christensen, L. (2000). *Reading, writing, and rising up: Teaching about social justice and the power of the written word.* Milwaukee: Rethinking Schools.

Christensen, L. (2009). *Teaching for joy and justice: Re-imagining the language arts classroom.* Milwaukee: Rethinking Schools.

Curtis, C. P. (1999). *Bud, not buddy.* New York: Random House.

Darling-Hammond, L. (2010). *Performance counts: Assessment systems that support high-quality learning.* Washington, DC: Council of Chief State School Officers.

Dyson, A. H. (1993). *Social worlds of children learning to write in an urban primary school.* New York: Teachers College Press.

Dyson, A. H. (1997). *Writing superheroes: Contemporary childhood, popular culture, and classroom literacy.* New York: Teachers College Press.

Edelsky, C. (1986). *Writing in a bilingual program: Había una vez.* Norwood, NJ: Ablex.

Edelsky, C. (1989). Putting language variation to work for you. In P. Rigg & V. G. Allen (Eds.), *When they don't all speak English: Integrating the ESL student into the regular classroom* (pp. 96–107). Urbana, IL: NCTE.

Fleischman, P. (2004). *Seedfolks* (Illus. D. Pedersen; Rev. HarperTrophy ed.). New York: HarperTrophy.

Fletcher, R. J. (1992). *What a writer needs.* Portsmouth, NH: Heinemann.

Fletcher, R. J. (2002). *Poetry matters: Writing a poem from the inside out.* New York: HarperCollins.

Franklin, E. (1989). Encouraging and understanding the visual and written works of second language children. In P. Rigg & V. G. Allen (Eds.), *When they don't all speak English: Integrating the ESL student into the regular classroom* (pp. 77–95). Urbana, IL: NCTE.

Freire, P., & Macedo, D. P. (1995). A dialogue: Culture, language, and race. *Harvard Educational Review, 65*(3), 377–402.

Fu, D. (2003). *An island of English: Teaching ESL in Chinatown.* Portsmouth, NH: Heinemann.

Fu, D. (2009). *Writing between languages: How English language learners make the transition to fluency, grades 4–12.* Portsmouth, NH: Heinemann.

Garcia, A., & Chiki, F. (April, 2010a). 21st century literacies: Online learning and students with special needs. *School Talk, 15*(3).

Garcia, A., & Chiki, F. (January, 2010b). 21st century literacies: Young children reading and writing in a digital world. *School Talk, 15*(2).

Garza, C. L., Rohmer, H., & Alarcón, F. X. (2000). *In my family/En mi familia.* San Francisco: Children's Book Press.

Gee, J. P. (1996). *Social linguistics and literacies: Ideology in discourses.* Critical perspectives on literacy and education (2nd ed.). Philadelphia: Falmer.

Goldberg, N. (2010). *Writing down the bones: Freeing the writer within.* Boston: Shambhala Publications.

Graham, S. (2006). Strategy instruction and the teaching of writing: A meta-analysis. In C. A. MacArthur, S. Graham, & J. Fitzgerald (Eds.), *Handbook of writing research* (pp. 187–207). New York: Guilford Press.

Graves, D. H. (1983). *Writing: Teachers and children at work.* Portsmouth, NH: Heinemann.

Graves, D. H. (1994). *A fresh look at writing.* Portsmouth, NH: Heinemann.

Harste, J. C., & Short, K. G. (with Burke, C. L.). (1988). *Creating classrooms for authors: The reading-writing connection.* Portsmouth, NH: Heinemann.

Haven, C. (2009, October 12). The new literacy: Stanford study finds richness and complexity in students' writing. *Stanford Report.* Retrieved from http://news.stanford.edu/news/2009/october12/lunsford-writing-research-101209.html.

Heard, G. (1995). *Writing toward home: Tales and lessons to find your way.* Portsmouth, NH: Heinemann.

Heard, G. (1999). *Awakening the heart: Exploring poetry in elementary and middle school.* Portsmouth, NH: Heinemann.

Heath, S. (1983). *Ways with words: Language, life, and work in communities and classrooms.* Cambridge, UK: Cambridge University Press.

Heffernan, L. (2004). *Critical literacy writer's workshop: Bringing purpose and passion to student writing*. Newark, DE: International Reading Association.

Heffernan, L., & Lewison, M. (2003). Social narratives: (Re) constructing kid culture. *Language Arts, 80*(6), 435–443.

Hertzog, N. B. (2001). Reflections and impressions from Reggio Emilia: It's not about the art. *Early Childhood Research and Practice, 3*(1), http://ecrp.uiuc.edu/v3n1/hertzog.html.

Holm, J. L., & Holm, M. (2005). *Babymouse: Queen of the world!* Babymouse, 1. New York: Random House.

Johnson, N.J., and Chiki, F. (January, 2009a). Nurturing our very youngest writers. *School Talk, 14*(2).

Johnson, N. J., and Chiki, F. (April, 2009b). Writing in the content areas: Making it real, making it theirs. *School Talk, 14*(3).

Kajder, S. B. (2010). *Adolescents and digital literacies: Learning alongside our students*. Urbana, IL: NCTE.

Kress, G. R. (1997). *Before writing: Rethinking the paths to literacy*. New York: Routledge.

Laman, T., & Van Sluys, K. (2008). Being and becoming: Multilingual writers' practices. *Language Arts, 85*(4), 265–274.

Lyons, G. E. (1999). *Where I'm from: Where poems come from*. Spring, TX: Absey.

Miller, D. (2002). *Reading with meaning: Teaching comprehension in the primary grades*. Portland, ME: Stenhouse.

Mills, H., Jennings, L. B., Donnelley, A., Mueller, L. Z. (2001). When teachers have time to talk: The value of curricular conversations. *Language Arts, 79*(1), 20–28.

Mills, H., O'Keefe, T., & Jennings, L. B. (2004). *Looking closely and listening carefully: Learning literacy through inquiry*. Urbana, IL: NCTE.

Moll, L. (2001). The diversity of schooling: A cultural-historical approach. In M. de la Luz Reyes & J. J. Halcón (Eds.), *The best for our children: Critical perspectives on literacy for Latino students*. New York: Teachers College Press.

Myers, W. D. (2009). *Looking like me*. New York: Egmont USA.

National Council of Teachers of English (NCTE). (2007). Framing statements on assessment. *National Council of Teachers of English*. March 1, 2010. Retrieved from http://www.ncte.org/positions/statements/assessmentframingst

National Council of Teachers of English and International Reading Association (NCTE–IRA). (1996). *Standards for the English language arts*. Urbana, IL: NCTE and Newark, DE: IRA.

NCTE/IRA Joint Task Force on Assessment. (2010). *Standards for the assessment of reading and writing* [Rev. ed.]. Newark, DE: International Reading Association and Urbana, IL: National Council of Teachers of English. Retrieved from http://www.ncte.org/standards/assessmentstandards/task-force

Nieto, S., & Bode, P. (2008). *Affirming diversity: The sociopolitical context of multicultural education* (5th ed.). Boston: Pearson/Allyn and Bacon.

Nye, N. S. (2005). *19 varieties of gazelle: Poems of the Middle East*. New York: HarperCollins.

Nye, N. S. (2008). *Honeybee: Poems and short prose*. New York: Greenwillow.

Nye, N. S. (2010). *Time you let me in: 25 poets under 25*. New York: Greenwillow.

Nye, N. S., & Maher, T. (2005). *A maze me: Poems for girls*. New York: Greenwillow.

Nye, N. S., & Yaccarino, D. (2000). *Come with me: Poems for a journey*. New York: Greenwillow.

Owocki, G., & Goodman, Y. M. (2002). *Kidwatching: Documenting children's literacy development*. Portsmouth, NH: Heinemann.

Pennypacker, S. (2006). *Clementine*. New York: Hyperion.

Pritchard, R. J., & Honeycutt, R. L. (2006). The process approach to writing instruction: Examining its effectiveness. In C. A. MacArthur, S. Graham, & J. Fitzgerald (Eds.), *Handbook of writing research* (pp. 187–207). New York: Guilford Press.

Ray, K. W. (1999). *Wondrous words: Writers and writing in the elementary classroom*. Urbana, IL: NCTE.

Ray, K. W., & Cleaveland, L. B. (2004). *About the authors: Writing workshop with our youngest writers*. Portsmouth, NH: Heinemann.

Ray, K. W., & Glover, M. (2008). *Already ready: Nurturing writers in preschool and kindergarten*. Portsmouth, NH: Heinemann.

Ray, K. W., & Laminack, L. L. (2001). *The writing workshop: Working through the hard parts (and they're all hard parts)*. Urbana, IL: NCTE.

Samway, K. D. (2006). *When English language learners write: Connecting research to practice, K–8*. Portsmouth, NH: Heinemann.

Short, K. G., & Harste, J. C. (with Burke, C. L.). (1996). *Creating classrooms for authors and inquirers*. Portsmouth, NH: Heinemann.

Spence, L. K. (2010). Generous reading: Seeing students through their writing. *Reading Teacher, 63*(8), 634–642.

Van Sluys, K. (2005). *What if and why? Literacy invitations for multilingual classrooms*. Portsmouth, NH: Heinemann.

Van Sluys, K., Cambron, Y., Perez, T., Garcia, C., Rosales, C., & Ramirez, A. (2008). Engaging as ethnographers: Insights from the collaborative study of a literacy learning community. *Voices from the Middle, 16*(1), 15–22.

Van Sluys, K., & Reinier, R. (2006). Seeing the possibilities: Learning from, with, and about multilingual classroom communities. *Language Arts, 83*(4), 321–331.

Vopat, J. (1994). *The parent project: A workshop approach to parent involvement*. York, ME: Stenhouse.

Weiser, M. E., Fehler, B. M., & González, A. M. (Eds.) (2009). *Engaging audience: Writing in an age of new literacies*. Urbana, IL: NCTE.

Wenger, E. (1999). *Communities of practice: Learning, meaning, and identity*. New York: Cambridge University Press.

Wilson, L. (2006). *Writing to live: How to teach writing in today's world*. Portsmouth, NH: Heinemann.

Index

Advocacy Day (NCTE), 129–30
Allen, JoBeth, 121
analysis and coding, 108–9
analysis of analysis, 100
anchor rubrics, 96
anecdotal notes, 103
Applegate, Katherine, 77
article writing for newsletters, 41–42
The Art of Teaching Writing (Calkins), 19
assessment
    checklists, 101–2
    feedback for growth, 109–10
    formative and summative, defined, xx
    and judgment, in *NCTE Beliefs*, xx
    note taking, 102–4
    observations for, 101–4
    on-demand, 98–100
    over time, 106–10
    overview, 91–94
    rubrics, 96–97, 105–7
    shared visions and, 94–98
    student reflections and rubrics, 104–6
    summative assessment and the grading dilemma, 110–13
Atwell, Nancie, 87, 135
audience
    feedback from, 43–44
    newsletters and, 41–42
    purpose, form, and, 31
    shaping readers' thinking, 44–47
authoring cycles, 19–20
authors and thinking behind the text, 76–77
awareness of thought processes. *See* metacognitive reflection

Barton, D., 8
beginning lines, using models for, 56–59
behind-the-text thinking, 75–78
beliefs about writing. *See* vision
"big ideas" talk, 119
bilingual classrooms and practices, 53–56, 122
blogging, 43
Bomer, Katherine, 18, 21, 135
Bomer, Randy, 8, 18, 21
Brown, Monica, 77
Bud, Not Buddy (Curtis), 29
bulletin board displays, 69
Burke, Carolyn, 18
Butterflies on Carmen Street (Brown), 77

Calkins, Lucy, 19
calling it quits vs. sticking with it, 75
carets, 59–61
charting
    stamina charts, 51–52
    Status of the Class charts, 87
    T-charts, 107–8
checklists, 101–2

choices, making and owning, 72–75
Choice Words (Johnston), 137
Christensen, Linda, 111, 119, 135
Clementine (Pennypacker), 76–77
coding and analysis, 108–9
coffee talks, 127–28
collaborations beyond the school. *See* outreach to stakeholders
    and constituencies
collegial collaborations, 116–21
community action projects, 129
community leaders, involving, 128–29
community outreach. *See* family and community collaborations
conditions for metacognitive reflection
    choices, making and owning, 72–75
    overview, 67
    perseverance and walking away, understanding, 75
    quality writing, understanding, 70–72
    supportive writing communities, 68–70
conditions for writing. *See* how writers write
conferences, 59–61, 84–86
constituencies. *See* outreach to stakeholders and constituencies
conventions of finished and edited texts, importance of, xiii–xv
Corgill, Ann Marie, 136
correspondence with families, 122–26
Creating Classrooms for Authors and Inquirers (Short & Harste), 20
Creating Critical Classrooms (Lewison, Leland, & Harste), 137
Creating Welcoming Schools (Allen), 121
curricular conversations, 119–20
curriculum meetings with families, 127–28
Curtis, Christopher Paul, 29

data gathering, 78
David, A. D., 8
"Dear Writer" letters, 124–25
debates on social issues, 114–15
decisions
    behind-the-text thinking, 75–78
    cases showing purpose ("why"), 33–47
        anticipating and seeking responses, 43–44
        communicating with newsletters, 41–42
        reading, questioning, and responding, 37–40
        reporting, 35–37
        shaping readers' thinking, 44–47
    cases showing tools, techniques, and practices ("how"), 47–64
        models, 56–59
        multiple languages, 53–56
        punctuation to control readings, 61–64
        revision tools, 59–61
        scheduling, 48–50
        taking responsibility, 50–53
    conditions for taking ownership of, 67–75
        choices and responsibility, 72–75
        knowing when to stick with it or walk away, 75
        quality writing, 70–72
        supportive writing communities, 68–70
    defined, 4

overview, 5–7, 27–28
purpose and form, connection between, 28–33
scaffolding reflections on, 78–90
    collaborative work, supporting, 83–87
    holistic reflection on process, 81–83
    plans, goals, and intended actions, 87–90
    revision decisions, 79–81
dialogue, creating spaces for, 115–16
discourses influencing vision, 22–25
documentation boards, 126–27
Dyson, Anne Haas, 17

Edelsky, Carole, 18
The Essential Don Murray (Newkirk & Miller), 137
Essential Linguistics (Freeman & Freeman), 136
evaluation. *See* assessment

family and community collaborations
    at-home written conversation notebooks, 69
    community scavenger hunts, 128
    documentation boards, 126–27
    library nights, 121–22
    politicians and community leaders, 128–30
    professional conversations, 127–28
    publication celebrations, 126
    weekly workshops, 122
    written correspondence, 122–26
feedback for growth, 109–10
Fleischman, Paul, 43
Fletcher, Ralph, 18, 119
form and purpose, 28–33
formative assessment, defined, xx. *See also* assessment
Freeman, David, 136
Freeman, Yvonne, 136
Freire, P., 116
A Fresh Look at Writing (Graves), 120, 136–37
Fu, Danling, 18, 136
"funds of knowledge," 124

Garza, Carmen Lomas, 122
genres and purpose, 28–33
Giovanni, Nikki, 119
goals and intended actions, 88–90
Goldberg, Natalie, 120
grading dilemma, 110–13. *See also* assessment
Graves, Donald H., 18, 19, 120, 136–37

Hamilton, M., 8
Harste, Jerome, 8, 18, 19–20, 137
Heard, Georgia, 119, 120
Heffernan, Lee, 18
Hidden Gems (Bomer), 135
history of writing pedagogy, 17–22
holistic reflection on process, 81–83
Home of the Brave (Applegate), 77
how writers write (tools, techniques, practices, and conditions)
    controlling readings with punctuation, 61–64
    making time for writing, 48–50
    overview, 47–48
    revision tools, 59–61
    taking responsibility for writing, 50–53

using models, 56–59
using multiple languages, 53–56

ideas, writing as source of, xi–xii
independence of student writers, 101
information gathering, 78
inherited practices, 22
In My Family/En Mi Familia (Garza, Rohmer, & Alarcón), 122
inquiry cycles, 19–20
Internet. *See* technologies and modalities of writing
Ivanič, R., 8

Johnston, Peter H., 137
journals, morning, 69. *See also* notebooks
judgments and assessment, xx

Kress, G. R., 8
Krull, Kathleen, 77

Laminack, Lester L., 20, 138
languages, 53–56, 122
learning by writing, ix–x
Leland, Christine, 137
Lessons That Change Writers (Atwell), 135
Lewison, Mitzi, 137
library nights, 121–22
life experiences, remembering and recording, 33–35
literacy, bilingual, 53–56
literacy, changing nature of, 7–8
logs, 109
Looking Like Me? (Myers), 77
Lyon, George Ella, 43–44

Macedo, D. P., 116
mapping software, 109
Mario Karts poem, 62–63
McNees, Kelly O'Connor, 77
media technology. *See* technologies and modalities of writing
metacognitive reflection
    behind-the-text thinking, learning to see, 75–78
    conditions for, 67–75
        choices, making and owning, 72–75
        perseverance vs. walking away, 75
        quality writing, understanding, 70–72
        writing communities, supportive, 68–70
    overview, 65–66
    scaffolding reflection on decisions, 78–90
        on collaborative work, 83–87
        plans, intentions, and actions, 87–90
        process, reflecting holistically on, 81–83
        on revision decisions, 79–81
Miller, Lisa, 137
mistakes, learning from, 68
modalities. *See* technologies and modalities of writing
models, 56–59
morning journals, 69
motivation to write, response from readers as, 43–44
Moyer, Bill, 119
Murray, Don, 18
Myers, Walter Dean, 77

National Council of Teachers of English (NCTE)
    Advocacy Day, 129–30
    annual legislative platform, 130
    importance of, 10
    NCTE Beliefs about the Teaching of Writing, ix–xxi, 10–13, 22, 130
    NCTE–IRA *Standards for the English Language Arts*, 117
National Day on Writing, 44
National Gallery of Writing, 28, 43–44
NCTE Beliefs about the Teaching of Writing, ix–xxi, 10–13, 22, 130
NCTE–IRA *Standards for the English Language Arts*, 117
Newkirk, Thomas, 137
newsletter article writing, 41–42
newspapers, 36
notebooks
    at-home written conversation notebooks, 69
    as space to react, 38
    vision and, 13
notes to students, personalized, 52
note taking, 102–4
Nye, Naomi Shihab, 21, 31, 119

observations as assessment for learning, 101–4
Of Primary Importance (Corgill), 136
Ok, H., 8
"on-demand" assessment, 98–100
outreach to stakeholders and constituencies
    collegial collaborations, 116–21
        curricular conversations, 119–20
        study groups, 120
        vertical team meetings, 120–21
    dialogue, creating spaces for, 115–16
    family and community collaborations, 121–30
        community scavenger hunts, 128
        documentation boards, 126–27
        library nights, 121–22
        politicians and community leaders, involving, 128–30
        professional conversations, 127–28
        publication celebrations, 126
        weekly workshops, 122
        written correspondence, 122–26
    overview, 114–15
ownership. *See* responsibility and ownership of writing

peer support and collaboration
    coding and analysis, 109
    constructing supportive writing communities, 68–70
    scaffolding, 83–87
peer text, thinking behind, 77–78
peer writing as model texts, 56–59
peer writing conferences, 84–86
Pennypacker, Sara, 76–77
perseverance, 75
personal narratives with "on-demand" assessment, 99
plans, 51, 87. *See also* decisions
poetry
    curricular conversations on, 119–20
    narrative self-reflection with, 104–6
    poetry pals across grades, 61–63
    punctuation to control readings, 61–64
    virtual communities and, 43–44
    worldviews and form vs. meaning, 21

politicians and community leaders, involving, 128–30
practices, writing. *See* how writers write
process approach
    context influences and, 22–23
    history of movement, 17
    holistic reflection on process, 81–83
    in *NCTE Beliefs*, x–xi
    workshops and authoring cycles, 18–20
professional conversations, 127–28
publication celebrations, 126
public service announcements (PSAs), 129
punctuation to control readings, 61–64
purpose
    anticipating and seeking response, 43–44
    form and, 28–33
    in *NCTE Beliefs*, xii–xiii
    newsletter article writing, 41–42
    reading, questioning, and responding practices, 37–40
    remembering and recording life experiences, 33–35
    reporting, 35–37
    shaping readers' thinking, 44–47

quality writing
    assessment and, 96, 112–13
    choice and, 72–75
    understanding, 70–72
questioning, 37–40
quotes to launch writing, 65–66, 70–71

Ray, Katie Wood, 19, 20, 120, 137–38
reacting, 37–40
reading
    reading, questioning, and responding practices, 37–40
    reporting from, 36
    thinking behind the text, 75–78
    writing, relationship with, xv–xvi, 36
recording life experiences, 33–35
reflection on thought processes. *See* metacognitive reflection
remembering life experiences, 33–35
reporting, 35–37
responding practices, 37–40
response from readers, 43–44
responsibility and ownership of writing
    choices, making and owning, 72–75
    holistic reflection on process, 81–83
    knowing what to do, when, and why, 50–53
    metacognitive reflection and, 67
revision, 59–61, 79–81
risk taking, 68–69
Routman, Regie, 138
rubrics, 96–97, 105–7

scaffolding
    collaborative work, 83–87
    creating supportive contexts, 78
    plans, intentions, and actions, 87–90
    reflecting holistically on process, 81–83
    revision decisions, 79–81
    starts, 52
Scales, Bobby, 45
scavenger hunts, community, 128
scheduling, 48–50

School Talk, 120
"Second Grade Scoop" newsletter, 41–42
Seedfolks (Fleischman), 43
self-assessment, 104–6
Short, Kathy, 18, 19–20
social and cultural dimensions of writing, 17–18, 20–21
social issues debates, 114–15
social issues writing, 30–33
social relationships as context for writing, xvii–xviii
Spence, Lucy, 99
stakeholders. *See* outreach to stakeholders and constituencies
stamina charts, 51–52
Stanford Study of Writing, 8
Status of the Class charts, 87
step-by-step approach, 70
sticking with it vs. calling it quits, 75
strategies for writing. *See* how writers write
study groups, 120
summative evaluation, xx, 110–13

talk
    on punctuation decisions, 63–64
    videos for "how writers talk," 86
    and writing, relationship between, in *NCTE Beliefs*, xvi–xvii
T-charts, 107–8
Teaching for Joy and Justice (Christensen), 119, 135
team meetings, vertical, 120–21
techniques for writing. *See* how writers write
technologies and modalities of writing
    blogging, 43
    connecting with authors, 77
    literacy and, 8
    in *NCTE Beliefs*, xviii–xix
    virtual writing communities and response as motivation, 43–44
testing, state, 130
thinking, writing as tool for, xi–xii
thinking behind-the-text, 75–78
thought processes, reflection on. *See* metacognitive reflection
time for writing, scheduling, 48–50, 69
Tomás the Take-Home Tiger, 123–24
tools for writing. *See* how writers write
"track changes," 108

vertical team meetings, 120–21
video cameras, 86
virtual writing communities, 43–44
vision
    assessment and, 92, 94–98
    change and, 7–8
    constituencies and range of, 114
    current beliefs, 8–10
    current instructional and learning practices, 11
    and history of writing pedagogy, 17–22
    NCTE Beliefs about the Teaching of Writing, ix–xxi, 10–13, 22, 130
    overview, 4–7
    purpose and, 32–33
    shared mission or vision statements, 117–18
    worldviews and discourses influencing, 21, 22–25
"voice," xvi

walking away from a piece, 75
What a Writer Needs (Fletcher), 18
What You Know by Heart (Ray), 137–38
"Where I'm From" (Lyon), 43–44
Wilson, Lorraine, 20–21
Wondrous Words (Ray), 120
workshops
    with family members, 122
    writing workshops, 19, 22–23
worldviews, 21, 22–25
World Writing, 30–33
write-arounds, 29, 30
writerly language, 62
Writing between Languages (Fu), 136
writing centers, 49
Writing Essentials (Routman), 138
Writing Workshop, The (Ray & Laminack), 138
writing workshops, 19, 22–23
written conversation notebooks, at-home, 69

Zoch, M. P., 8
"zooming in" on revisions, 79–81

Author

Katie Van Sluys is an associate professor of literacy at DePaul University. Her work as a teacher, learner, and person is closely tied to the everyday lives of children and teachers as she works with school communities in capacities ranging from side-by-side learner, on-site university course instructor, literacy coach, student teacher advisor, study group facilitator, and literacy researcher. Van Sluys's interest in the development of literate lives grows from her work as an elementary teacher in multilingual, international, rural, suburban, and urban contexts, and her interests lead her to work with multilingual learners, writing pedagogy and practice, critical and 21st century literacies, and learning communities dedicated to lifelong, life-wide growth for young people and educators alike. She is the author of *What If and Why? Literacy Invitations for Multilingual Classrooms* as well as numerous journal articles and book chapters.

This book was typeset in Janson Text and BotonBQ by
Barbara Frazier.

Typefaces used on the cover include American Typewriter,
Frutiger Bold, Formata Light, and Formata Bold.

The book was printed on 60-lb Recycled Offset paper
by Versa Press, Inc.

30% Total Recycled Fiber